MITCHELL BEAZLEY

PHIL VICKERY'S
FAVOURITE
THE BEST OF BRITISH COOKING
FOOD

PHOTOGRAPHY

CONTENTS

For Winnie and Grace, the chief tasters

Phil Vickery's Favourite Food

First published in Great Britain in 2007 as
Britain The Cookbook
by Mitchell Beazley, an imprint of Octopus
Publishing Group Limited,
2–4 Heron Quays, London E14 4JP.
An Hachette UK Company
www.hachette.co.uk

This paperback edition published in 2010

© Octopus Publishing Group Limited 2007
Text © Phil Vickery 2007
Photographs © Steve Lee 2007

ISBN: 978 1 845335 540

While all reasonable care has been taken during
the preparation of this edition, the publisher,
editors or the author cannot accept responsibility
for any consequences arising from the use
thereof or from the information contained
therein.

Commissioning Editor: Rebecca Spry
Art Director: Tim Foster
Design: Miranda Harvey
Editorial Consultant: Simon Whittaker
Editors: Susan Fleming, Martyn Page
Proofreader: Debbie Robertson
Home Economist: Julia Alger
Production: Peter Hunt
Index: Diana LeCore

Typeset in Quadraat and Grotesque
Printed and bound by Toppan, China

INTRODUCTION

A mixture of personal interest and an ever-depleting larder, not to mention the quest for perfection, drew me towards the people and places featured in this book: some of the very best of Britain's food producers and suppliers.

I have travelled all over the UK and met some amazing characters, all united in the desire to grow, produce or catch the best food possible. I have made many friends, and I have served the wonderful produce of most in my restaurants and pubs. I am delighted to say the producers' passion has been matched by an appreciative dining clientele hungry to snap up whatever they produce.

Every producer in this book has been going about their own brand of food-business for years. Several of the family producers featured have been in the same game for well over a century. I was also keen to discover and show the unique (and at times archaic) methods that many of them have evolved over time to make their products the best around.

Most artisan food-producers have had some tough times over the years. All businesses go through ups and downs, but one thing this lot share is their steadfast, unshakeable belief in their products, which they have stuck to through thick and thin. Now there is renewed public interest in artisan-made quality food, many of our producers are back on an even keel.

From a chef's point of view, it has been an incredible journey and in most cases I have had the privilege of experiencing this food in a hands-on manner. What better way is there to assess how well something is produced? I have made cheese with award-winner Todd Trethowan in Wales, wild boar sausages with Peter Gott in Cumbria, and a decent fist of seaside rock with Roy, a master of this deceptively difficult task in Great Yarmouth. I've caught Cromer crabs with fishermen Gary Meers and Richard Matthews in Norfolk, plus I spent a day with Terry, the 'sea dog' pilchard salter in Cornwall.

But the best experience of all, which simply had to be in this book even though it didn't happen in Britain, has to have been venturing deep into the southern Irish countryside to collect honey with Philip McCabe, a master of his craft, and afterwards taking

afternoon tea with 20 beekeeping nuns in a nearby convent. The youngest of the nuns was over 60 years of age, and they were the most delightful group of ladies you could hope to meet. Not only that, I have to say as a time-served pastry chef that their honey- and cream-laden scones put mine to shame!

This fabulous experience has really made me think about, feel for and cook food in a different light. So in the following chapters I have come up with a selection of recipes that incorporate the best British foods I have seen and had the honour of helping produce. My modest aim for these simple, tasty recipes is to bring out the best in their unique ingredients.

On a final, but nevertheless for me very important, note, I have personally researched and created all the recipes. I have also prepared and cooked every one of the dishes in this book at least once, some hundreds of times, so I know they will work for you – something that I'm particularly proud of.

Enjoy cooking and eating!

Phil Vickery

THE WEST
COUNTRY

SARDINES
CORNISH SARDINES

The August evening when I arrived in Newlyn, the sea was dead flat, like a sheet of turquoise glass. Just as well, because I was looking for a fishing boat to join its crew in pursuit of that ancient Cornish prey, the pilchard (a mature or grown-up sardine).

Stefan Glinsky and his two-man crew go out in all winds and weathers in the Pride of Cornwall. As we headed out into Mounts Bay, Stefan told me that only a century or so ago, pilchard shoals were so big they could be seen by the naked eye, flashing silver in the sea. Back then, open rowing boats were directed to their target by 'huers', sharp-eyed, cliff-top guides who used semaphore-style flags and sheer vocal power. These days Stefan has to make his own way with a little help from hi-tech equipment. His sonar can pick up the oxygen trapped in each fish's swim-bladder: the bigger the signal, the bigger the shoal.

A mile or so out, Stefan calmly showed me a five-ton shoal on screen. Action stations! The powerful deck-lights were cut, and Stefan cranked his boat round, feeding out his net in a huge ring as he circled the shoal. Having closed up the bottom of the net, they began the process of hauling the huge purse-net back in. The smaller the purse became, the more racket the gulls made, and then you could actually see Stefan's first catch of the night, darting this way and that in quicksilver streaks.

I thought they'd just haul the net in and drop the three-quarter ton catch into the hold. Instead, Stefan uses a huge metal ladle to delicately transfer the fish into slush-ice so as not to damage them.

At the time of my visit, in August 2005, Stefan's biggest customer was the Cornish Fish Works in Newlyn, a working museum that had been processing and preserving Cornish pilchards since the 1920s. (Sadly, though, mirroring what's happening all over Cornwall, it is now a block of apartments.) Its owner, Nick Howell, had done a lot to keep the traditional pilchard industry going in Cornwall, not least by bringing modern-day marketing nous to this ancient trade. His biggest coup had been re-branding pilchards as 'Cornish sardines'. That one verbal flourish increased his sales a hundredfold as customers who'd long ago turned their back on canned fish were won over again and persuaded to buy what are perceived to be fillets of sophisticated Mediterranean food.

What the tourists really came to see at Nick Howell's place was the ancient art of preserving pilchards in salt. The fish were immersed whole in French sea salt for up to two years at a time, the salt both killing all the germs and flavouring the fish. To demonstrate, Nick unearthed a two-year-old pilchard from the salt, set to with a penknife, and we had an impromptu snack of what tasted deliciously like anchovies.

While we were there, Terry, Nick's 'apprentice now retired', showed me how he loaded the salted fish into 'coffins' – big wooden cases – that were pressed in a vice to squeeze any last traces of oil and liquid out of the pilchards. The fish were then packed in stencilled wooden crates and shipped off to eager buyers in Italy and Spain just as they have been from Cornwall for the past half millennium.

Tragically, this last vestige of the old Cornwall has now gone for ever. I am so glad I managed to catch it.

August – Terry packed the salted sardines into wooden 'coffins' before we strolled round Newlyn Harbour on a beautiful sunny day

SARDINE AND SPICY TOMATO TOASTS

Great cooking consists of simple things put together carefully, and this recipe is a prime example of that. If you are lucky enough to have tomatoes in your greenhouse they are perfect for this simple treatment.

1 For the dressing, heat 2 tbsp of the olive oil, add the garlic and shallots and cook gently for 3-4 minutes to soften slightly, then cool.

2 Once the garlic and shallots have cooled, place them in a large bowl. Add the tarragon, remaining olive oil, sunflower oil, sherry vinegar, salt and pepper, and mix well.

3 Add the sun-blush and fresh tomatoes to the bowl, re-season with salt and pepper and mix well.

4 Char-grill the crusty bread. Cut each slice on the diagonal then rub with a little cut garlic.

5 To serve, warm the sardines under a grill or in a warm oven; do not overheat. Place on to the grilled bread, then spoon over the dressing and liberally sprinkle with chopped parsley.

Serves: 4

2 x 100g (3½oz) cans smoked sardines, drained

4 slices crusty bread

2 cloves of garlic, peeled

A handful of chopped parsley

Tomato dressing

6 tbsp extra virgin olive oil

1 garlic clove, peeled and crushed

4 shallots, peeled and finely chopped

2 tbsp chopped tarragon

2 tbsp sunflower oil

2 tbsp sherry vinegar

salt and freshly ground black pepper

115g (4oz) sun-blush tomatoes, roughly chopped

4 ripe tomatoes on the vine, roughly chopped

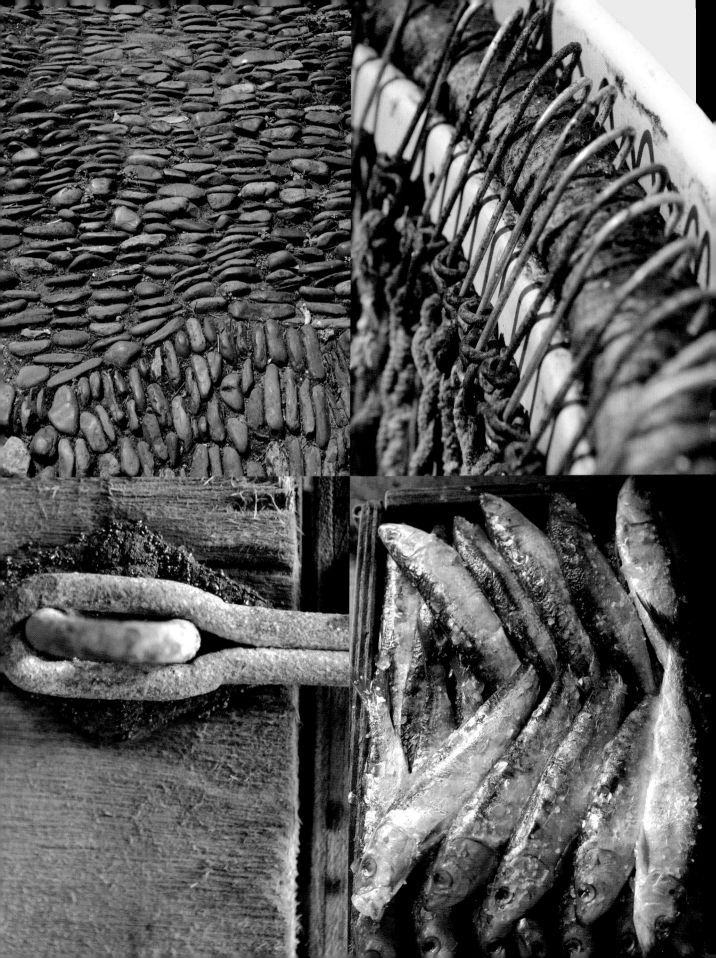

HERBY SARDINE PASTA BAKE

Pasta bakes are easy to make. They can be made well in advance, chilled and reheated for a quick supper.

Serves: 4

2 tbsp vegetable oil

1 small onion, peeled and finely sliced

1 garlic clove, peeled and crushed

55g (2oz) unsalted butter

55g (2oz) plain flour

600ml (1 pint) full-fat milk, boiled and hot

2 tbsp wholegrain mustard

100g (3½oz) mascarpone

115g (4oz) Cheddar, roughly grated

about 500g (18oz) cooked farfalle, rigatoni or penne (raw, 300g/10 ½oz approx.)

4 tbsp each of roughly chopped parsley and basil

salt and freshly ground black pepper

2 x 100g (3½oz) cans smoked sardines, drained

1 Preheat the oven to 200°C/400°F/Gas 6. Heat the vegetable oil in a saucepan, add the onion and garlic, and cook for 5 minutes to soften, then cool.

2 Melt the butter in a separate saucepan, then stir in the flour. Gradually add the hot milk, and bring to the simmer, stirring all the time. Stir in the onion and garlic and the mustard.

3 Pour the hot sauce into a bowl, and add the mascarpone, 85g (3oz) of Cheddar, the cooked pasta, basil and parsley. Season well and mix together. Spoon a layer of the pasta mixture into a baking dish, roughly 20 x 30 x 7cm (7 x 12 x 3in). Lay on the pilchards, then cover with the rest of the pasta. Top with the remaining Cheddar, then place on a baking tray. Bake for about 20 minutes. Cool slightly, then serve with a dressed green salad and garlic bread.

BROCCOLI WITH SARDINE AND GARLIC DRESSING

I love this dish. If fresh wild garlic leaves are not available, replace with 2 crushed garlic cloves, 2 tbsp roughly chopped baby spinach and 2 tbsp roughly chopped fresh basil.

Serves: 4

500g (18oz) purple sprouting or tender-stem broccoli

salt and freshly ground black pepper

Dressing

2 x 100g (3½oz) cans sardines, drained and very finely chopped

6 tbsp extra virgin olive oil

a pinch of caster sugar

2 tbsp roughly chopped parsley

4 tbsp roughly chopped wild garlic leaves

4 tbsp finely chopped wild rocket

3 tbsp pine nuts, lightly toasted

1 For the dressing, place the chopped sardines, 4 tbsp of the olive oil, the sugar and a little pepper in a bowl and mix well. Add the parsley, wild garlic, rocket and pine nuts, then mix well again. It's best to leave the dressing for about 2 hours if you can.

2 Trim the broccoli, discarding all but a few leaves. Any stalks that are a little thick can be split down the middle so you end up with all the stalks roughly the same size (the leaves can be cooked separately and eaten at a different meal). Cook the broccoli for 5-6 minutes in plenty of boiling salted water and drain well. Do not allow to overcook. Keep warm.

3 Add 1 tbsp cold water and the remaining olive oil to the dressing. Pile the warm broccoli on to plates and spoon over the dressing. Leave for 2-3 minutes, then eat.

SARDINE, MUSHROOM AND SPRING ONION TART

A little goes a long way in this recipe. The full, powerful flavour of the sardines is great. It makes a good summer starter or main course; I like to serve it with a ripe tomato salad, at room temperature.

Serves: 6

Pastry

250g (9oz) plain flour

salt, to taste

125g (4½oz) cold butter, diced

(or 1 x 28cm (11in) circle ready-rolled shortcrust pastry)

Filling

20g (¾oz) dried cep mushrooms

1-2 tbsp olive oil

2 large spring onions, peeled and chopped

1 garlic clove, peeled and crushed

2 medium eggs, plus 1 medium egg yolk

400ml (14fl oz) full-cream milk

4 tbsp chopped parsley

½ tsp ground coriander

salt and freshly ground black pepper

2 x 100g (3½oz) cans sardines, drained and broken into small pieces

1 If you're making your own pastry, put the flour in a shallow bowl, then add a pinch of salt and the butter. Rub in the butter until you have a soft breadcrumb texture. Add enough water to bring together to a firm dough. Refrigerate for an hour.

2 Preheat the oven to 200°C/400°F/Gas 6.

3 Grease a loose-bottomed flan tin, 20cm (8in) in diameter, 4cm (1½in) deep. Roll out the pastry on a lightly floured surface to a 28cm (11in) circle. Line the tin with the pastry. Bake blind for about 15-20 minutes until the pastry is set but not overcooked.

4 Meanwhile, soak the mushrooms in boiling water for about 15 minutes, or until soft, then drain and squeeze out any excess liquid. If they look gritty, rinse again.

5 Heat the oil in a frying pan, add the onion and garlic and cook until soft and lightly golden.

6 Whisk together the eggs, egg yolk, milk, parsley and coriander and season well.

7 Spread the chopped sardines, onion and garlic over the base of the tart, then lay the mushrooms on top. Pour in enough of the egg mixture to fill the tart about three-quarters full. Place the tart in the oven then, using a small cup, add more of the egg mixture so the tart is full.

8 Bake for about 35 minutes, or until just very slightly runny in the centre. The residual heat will finish it off perfectly.

9 Allow to cool completely, then cut into big wedges and serve.

CIDER
SHEPPY'S CIDER

If I mention 'King's Favourite', 'Crimson King' or 'Lorna Doone', you might think I'm talking about racehorses, pantomime characters or, at a push, 19th-century novels... Nope, they're apples – beautiful, uniquely British, apples!

The UK is home to over 6,000 varieties of apple, some of them now incredibly rare and limited to just one hedgerow or even, in some desperate cases, one lone tree. In Hereford, Worcestershire and the West Country, despite the best efforts of the EU to bribe farmers to grub up their trees, apple orchards still abound. As I drove down to an old stamping ground of mine in Somerset, the gnarled ranks of mature apple trees, their twisted trunks plastered with moss and lichen, were a delight to the eye.

My destination was Sheppy's cider farm, a stone's throw from Taunton. Having cooked with, as well as drunk plenty of, Sheppy's cider when I worked in Taunton, it was nice to come and see the process from start to finish for the very first time. We arrived in October, just the right time of year to see Sheppy's apples harvested, chopped and pressed.

Cider apples are very different from the cookers and eaters that most of us grow or buy. By and large they are smaller than shop apples – like crab-apples with attitude – but intensely flavoured, which comes in handy when it comes to fermentation.

Of the 30 apple varieties the Sheppy family can rely on every autumn, the most famous are the medium-dry Tremlett's Bitter, the mouth-puckeringly sharp Kingston Black, and the medium-sweet Dabinett and Taylor's Gold. Blending the different crops, with their unique flavour attributes, in vast quantities is a matter of judgement, experience and not a little skill, all of which David Sheppy has in spades. This is not surprising as his is a family business with generations of know-how, and David himself has been making cider for 20 years.

The process of turning apples into juice is ancient and was a real privilege for me to watch. The press used is a fine room-sized piece of Swiss-made precision machinery. The chopped apples are built up in cloth layers on a wooden grid, the one-tonne load being traditionally called a 'cheese', an appropriate name for the county that gave Cheddar to the world. The press then delivers 300 tonnes of pressure to the cheese, squeezing out 180 gallons of lovely clear apple juice at a time. (Sheppy's grows enough apples to make 90,000 gallons of cider each year.)

The magical process whereby apple juice transforms into notoriously potent alcohol happens in fermenting vats with little more than the yeast from the apples and time. Fermentation is an imprecise science and sometimes, though rarely, the fermentation and strength need a bit of helping along with some yeast. More often than not, though, ciders do perfectly well left to their own devices in the vats, and actually need diluting with water to bring them down to acceptable but still pokey strengths.

Fermentation takes a matter of a few weeks, after which the cider is kept in the vats to mature for about 3–4 months (depending on weather conditions), then it's bottled and that's it. The wonderful appley, earthy smell around the whole farm during cider-making time is quite overpowering but very evocative.

A few weeks later, as an experiment in cross-cultural pollination, I took some bottles of Sheppy's medium-sweet Dabinett cider to Norway for a chef's demonstration. It was alien to them but a real hit – in all senses of the word. I suggest you try it yourselves.

October - We picked hundreds of apples off the grass in the orchard. A dry year meant they were smaller than usual.

CIDER-MARINATED SALMON WITH CELERIAC AND PARSLEY SALAD

Serves: 4

200ml (7fl oz) apple cider

100ml (3½fl oz) apple juice

salt and freshly ground black pepper

1 tbsp caster sugar

500g (18oz) salmon fillet, cut into 4 equal pieces

a pinch of red chilli flakes (optional)

4 tbsp extra virgin olive oil (optional)

Celeriac and parsley salad

a squeeze of lemon juice

1 celeriac head, about 500g (18oz), peeled and cut into matchstick-sized pieces

½ garlic clove, peeled and finely chopped

4 tbsp chopped parsley

6 tbsp mayonnaise

The secret to this dish is to not overcook the salmon. There is enough residual heat in the pan to finish off the salmon perfectly. The soft flesh combined with the crunch of the celeriac salad works really well. It makes a great starter or lighter summer lunch.

1 Place the cider, apple juice, salt, pepper and sugar in a bowl and mix well. Add the salmon, ensuring it is all brushed with the marinade, cover, and leave in the fridge to marinate for 2 hours, or overnight if possible.

2 To start the salad, bring a pan of water to the boil and add 2 tsp salt and a dash of lemon juice. Bring back to the boil and plunge the celeriac in. Cook for 2 minutes, so it's cooked but not overcooked. Strain and refresh in cold water, then drain well. This is important as a lot of moisture will cling to the cooked celeriac.

3 Once well drained, place the celeriac in a bowl and add the garlic, parsley, and just enough mayonnaise to bind well. Season well with salt and pepper and some more lemon juice.

4 Take the salmon out of the marinade and place in a saucepan. Add half the marinade (discard the rest). Place the pan on the stove, bring to a gentle simmer, then turn off the heat and cover immediately. Leave for 10 minutes, and the fish will cook perfectly, provided the lid is left on. After 10 minutes (and the fish will be slightly undercooked, don't worry), remove the fish from the pan, and serve with the celeriac salad.

5 If you like, you can make an accompanying dipping sauce. Mix the chilli flakes and olive oil into the hot cider stock, and cook over a high heat for 3-4 minutes to reduce slightly and intensify the flavour. Once cooked down nicely, spoon into a bowl.

CIDER-MARINATED BARBECUED RABBIT WITH BRAMLEY APPLE GLAZE

Serves: 6

1 large rabbit, approx. 1.25kg (2 ¾lb), head on

salt and freshly ground black pepper

Brine

2.25 litres (3¾ pints) cold water

180g (6¼oz) table salt

55g (2oz) mustard seeds

190g (6¾oz) caster sugar

1 tbsp dried thyme

1 tsp dried sage

1 tsp garlic powder

1 tsp fennel seeds

600ml (1 pint) apple juice

500ml (18fl oz) dry cider

Bramley glaze

2 tbsp olive oil

1 tsp hot chilli powder

1 small onion, peeled and finely chopped

4 garlic cloves, peeled

100ml (3½fl oz) each of water, mirin (rice wine) and cider vinegar

500g (18oz) Bramley apples, cored and peeled

a little sugar to taste

This recipe is well worth the effort: the meat will fall off the bone and be very moist and tasty. The first thing is to brine the rabbit, which has to be done the day before. This helps soften the texture of the meat, and gives it a sweet and salty edge. The second stage is to cook it at a strictly controlled temperature, in this case 180°C/350°F: any hotter and the meat dries out and will toughen. You can cook at a much lower temperature, say at 120°C/250°F, which will extend the cooking time by probably 1-1¼ hours, and the end result will be just as spectacular. (Don't cook any slower than that, though.)

1 Put all the brine ingredients, apart from the apple juice and cider, in a large pan, bring to the boil, then leave to cool. Strain out all the seeds and dried herbs, and put the brine in a plastic, stainless-steel, ceramic or glass bowl. Once the brine is cool, add the apple juice and cider, then the rabbit. To make sure the rabbit is completely immersed in the brine, put a small plate on top of it. Cover and chill well for 12 hours, turning after 6. Drain the rabbit well and pat dry with kitchen towel, then season well with freshly milled black pepper.

2 To make the glaze, heat the oil in a saucepan, and add the chilli, onion and whole garlic cloves. Cook for 2 minutes to soften. Then add the water, mirin and vinegar and cook for a further 5 minutes. Add the chopped apples, a little sugar, and some salt and pepper. Bring to the boil and simmer for 15 minutes, or until pulpy. Liquidize and pass through a fine sieve. You should end up with a thick double cream consistency. The glaze will keep in the fridge for 3 weeks.

3 When ready to cook the rabbit, heat either the front or back burner of a gas barbecue, or one side of a charcoal barbecue, to 180°C/350°F. This is very important, and is known as cooking by an 'indirect' heat source. Place the whole rabbit on to the cool bars opposite the heated side or end. Put the lid on and cook for 30 minutes. Then, brush with the glaze. Repeat this process every 30 minutes (5 times), or every 20 minutes is just as good. Cook for 2½ hours in all, until cooked throughly. Also turn the rabbit occasionally. The secret is to keep the temperature constant at 180°C/350°F, so try and be quick when you are 'mopping'.

4 The meat will be soft and succulent, nicely coloured and very sweet. Serve ripped into large pieces, eaten with the fingers, with a little glaze.

This cider froth is perfect with roast apples or pears. It's also nice in the summer months with gooseberry compote, poached peaches or even fresh raspberries or mulberries. This simple but spectacular pudding only needs the addition of vanilla ice-cream or a little clotted cream.

ROAST APPLES AND PEARS WITH CIDER FROTH

Serves: 6

6 ripe firm British apples, such as Russet, Charles Ross, Worcester Pearmain

6 ripe Conference pears

4 tbsp olive oil

4 tbsp soft brown sugar

6 medium egg yolks

100g (3½oz) caster sugar

100ml (3½fl oz) cider

a squeeze of lemon juice

1 Preheat the oven to 200°C/400°F/Gas 6.

2 Cut all the fruit in half, and remove the cores. Leave the skins on. Place the fruits in a large bowl and mix with the olive oil and sugar before tipping into a baking tray or large ovenproof frying pan.

3 Place in the oven for 20 minutes, or until the fruit is soft, slightly puffy, but not overcooked. The fruit must remain whole. Turn occasionally, but try not to let the fruit break up.

4 Meanwhile, whisk the eggs, sugar and cider together over a pan of boiling water until thick and cooked. This will take 5-6 minutes. Finally add a squeeze of lemon juice. Do not overcook or the eggs will scramble. You will end up with a light frothy sauce. Once cooked, keep warm but not hot; I find it best to keep it warm in a Thermos flask, for a maximum of 1 hour.

5 To serve, spoon the hot fruit on to a large plate or bowl, then when ready pour over the froth. I like to serve this pudding with clotted cream and vanilla ice-cream: the hot and cold combination works really well.

EELS
BROWN & FORREST
AND BILLINGSGATE

Visiting London's famous Billingsgate fish market involves an early start even by a career chef's standards. I arrived there in the depths of winter at a gruesome 4am. Stallholders wisecracked at my expense at top volume as I stumbled half asleep through the stalls looking for the one, and only, Mick Jenrick.

Mick has been supplying London's 100 pie and mash shops with brown eels for the past 40 years. He started at the tender age of 17, as his mum and his dad were already in the business with a jellied-eel stand at the local dog track. Now he has a couple of lakes in East London where he stores all his eels, most coming from Ireland out of Loch Neagh, but in the winter months from the Netherlands. At those lakes they can fish as many as 15–20 tons per night.

Eel is treated as a delicacy in Japan and China, and these days the oriental restaurant trade is a large part of Mick's business. While we were chatting, a Chinese restaurateur stopped by to put in an order with Mick. 'They don't like the small 'uns, they want the big bastards,' says Mick.

He is larger then life and a very generous man. He gave me trays of eels, both jellied and fresh, which I cooked at home. Sadly, though, I had no takers round the table.

Mick's eels were sold to a famous pie and mash shop (sadly, now closed down) in Greenwich where I headed next after a hearty breakfast at Billingsgate's café. Goddard's pie and mash shop had been in Greenwich since 1890 and had survived the rage of the Luftwaffe and London's urban planners. Brothers Geoff and Kane Goddard gave me a warm welcome, a gravy-thick cuppa, then it was down to business for

a real lesson in proper pie, mash and that perennial accompanying 'liquor'. Except they wouldn't divulge their recipe for this thick whiteish sauce, no matter how much I begged them. I spent the morning with the brothers, even serving and delivering meals to the counter at one point during their mad lunchtime rush, but it was well worth the effort. They sold some 200 portions of Mick's warm boiled eels per day, all doused with liquor, plus a sprinkling of chilli vinegar.

A world away from the pearly kings and queens eating their jellied eels in steamy London cafés are the Somerset Levels in the West Country, a mysterious misty world of waterways, willows and meadows. Here in Langport is one firm whose approach to the humble eel is entirely different to that of Mick Jenrick. Brown & Forrest is a family firm, which seeks out and buys the river-dwelling silver eel from the idyllic chalk streams of Wiltshire, Hampshire and Dorset in order to smoke them.

Whereas Mick Jenrick's stock consists of lake-dwelling, bottom-feeding brown eels, fatty enough to create the jelly, the silver eel has lean, firm flesh from its annual travels to and from the far Sargasso Sea to spawn. Adult silver eels 'run' the rivers from July to December and Jesse Pattisson, who owns the Langport smokery, visits the riverbanks to buy his stock directly from the nets of elusive, shadowy river-keepers who make a living catching these eels.

Jesse's kiln can take 140 eels at a time and the process of preparing them is very quick compared to, say, salmon. Eels must be 'hot-smoked', i.e. cooked over a roaring open fire. This 'flash-cooking' takes a mere 15 minutes, after which the flames are doused with beech-wood shavings and dust. The resulting clouds of smoke give the eels their wonderful long-lasting flavour.

I can vouch for both Mick Jenrick eels and Brown & Forrest eels. Each is a truly fabulous product, prepared using ancient tried-and-tested methods. Our culinary landscape would unquestionably be a poorer place without them.

November—The smokery was packed with eels for the Christmas orders. I took one home and barbecued it for supper on Christmas day

WARM SMOKED EEL, CRISPY BACON AND CHICORY SALAD

This is a very simple salad to prepare. The secrets are not to cut the chicory too early or it will discolour; to get a nice colour on the potatoes; and to only just warm the eel. I think the less you muck about with a beautiful ingredient like this the better. The food will do the talking for you.

Serves: 4

about 20 baby new potatoes, peeled and freshly boiled

200g (7oz) British watercress

2 heads Belgian chicory, finely shredded

2 tbsp vegetable oil

12 rashers rindless streaky bacon, cut into 2cm (¾in) pieces

400g (14oz) smoked eel, skinned, boned, heads removed, cut into strips

Dressing

6 tbsp good-quality extra virgin olive oil

4 tsp wholegrain mustard

a pinch of caster sugar

juice of 1 lemon

salt and freshly ground black pepper

1 Preheat the oven to about 180°C/350°F/Gas 4, or preheat the grill.

2 Cut the potatoes in half lengthways and keep warm. Place the watercress and chicory in a large bowl.

3 Heat the vegetable oil in a wok, add the bacon and cook slowly for about 10-15 minutes, or until it starts to crisp up. Add the potatoes and cook until they are golden brown all over.

4 Meanwhile, mix together the dressing ingredients. Pour half the dressing over the leaves and toss well. Pile equal amounts of the potato and bacon mixture on to serving plates, then pile the salad leaves on top.

5 Warm the eel fillets through under the grill or in the oven for about 4-5 minutes, but do not overheat. Place two pieces of eel on top of each salad. Serve straightaway with the other half of the dressing spooned over the plates.

The oiliness of eel makes it ideal for the barbecue. You can use the packs of skinned, filleted, smoked eels you get from delis and supermarkets if you prefer.

The delicate flavour of the smoked fish can easily match up to the strong 'jerking' of the spices and sauce in this recipe. Jamaicans love jerk chicken and fish, the 'jerk' consisting of a combination of spices, some hot, with brown sugar and cinnamon. This, I believe, is one of the tastiest recipes I have ever come up with and, wait for it, even my children like it! Mind you, they didn't see the whole fish...

BARBECUED SMOKED EEL, JERK-STYLE

Serves: 4

1 x 500g (18oz) smoked eel, skinned, but head on

Jerk rub

1 tbsp onion salt

1 tbsp crispy fried onion flakes

1 tsp garlic powder

1 tsp ground allspice

1 tsp freshly ground black pepper

½ tsp cayenne pepper

2 tsp soft brown sugar

1 tsp dried thyme

½ tsp ground cinnamon

¼ tsp freshly grated nutmeg

¼ tsp red, hot chilli powder

½ tsp ground mace

Jerk fish sauce

300ml (10fl oz) water

1 fish stock cube

2 tbsp runny honey

3 tbsp tamarind paste

1 tbsp finely chopped fresh root ginger

a pinch of paprika to improve colour

1 heaped tbsp jerk rub

1 tbsp cornflour slaked with 4 tbsp cold water

1 Cut the eel in half, and half again, so you have a head section, a tail section and two middle sections. Leave the centre bone in.

2 Mix the jerk rub ingredients together well. You may need to break them up in a pestle. (Make well in advance and store until needed.) Pat most (leaving a tbsp for the sauce) over the fish and leave covered in the fridge for a couple of hours, or overnight if possible.

3 For the sauce, mix all the ingredients together, apart from the cornflour, and simmer until you have lost about a third. Blend the cornflour and water into the gently simmering liquid, and cook until thickened, about 15 minutes. Divide the sauce in two, one for brushing over the fish, one for dipping the cooked fish into.

4 Heat the barbecue until the coals are grey, or if you are using a gas barbecue, use a medium to low heat. Place the marinated eel on to the hot bars. Resist the temptation to move for 5 minutes, or the fish will stick well. After 5 minutes, brush liberally with the sauce, then leave again for 5 minutes. Carefully turn the fish over (the oils will now be flowing from the fish). Brush with more sauce and cook for 5 minutes. Finally turn the fish again just to brown the sauce. Take care, as the eel will burn if the barbie is too hot.

5 Serve straight from the barbecue, dipped into the remaining sauce, then eat with the fingers. Fantastic!

Michael Brown once said he could not only tell me the rivers the eels came from, but the specific beat. Very impressive. I devised this recipe using eels from the River Test for the BBC some years ago. At the time I put it on the menu and it sold really well, and has done so ever since.

BAKED SMOKED EEL PIE

Serves: 6

2 large carrots, peeled

2 large onions, peeled

2 large leeks, trimmed and well rinsed

2 large potatoes, peeled

450g (1lb) mussels, cleaned

50ml (2fl oz) white wine

2 large smoked eels, 450g (1lb) each, skinned, boned and heads removed

3 tbsp vegetable oil

salt and freshly ground black pepper

300ml (10fl oz) fish stock

55g (2oz) unsalted butter, cubed

1 large sheet ready-rolled puff pastry

1 medium egg, beaten

1 Preheat the oven to 200°C/400°F/Gas 6.

2 Cut the vegetables into 1.5cm (⅝in) cubes and cook in separate pans of boiling water until tender, then drain well.

3 Check the mussels and discard any that are open and do not close when tapped on the work surface. Heat the wine in a pan, add the mussels and cover with a lid. Cook over a high heat for a few minutes until the mussels have opened. Discard any mussels that are still closed. Remove the mussel meat from the open shells.

4 Cut the eels into 5cm (2in) pieces. Heat the oil in a frying pan, add the eel pieces, and cook quickly to brown all over. Season well, then place in the bottom of a 24cm (9½in) square pie dish, about 4cm (1½in) deep. Scatter the vegetables over the eels and season, then add the mussels. Pour over the fish stock and dot with the butter.

5 Cut out a strip of pastry about 2cm (¾in) wide and press on to the rim of the pie dish. Then cut out an oval piece of pastry, which is just larger all round than the dish. Brush a little water over the pastry rim and top with the pastry lid. Press together to seal, then trim off excess pastry, knock up the edges and flute. Brush a little beaten egg over the lid and use a sharp knife to make a hole in the centre.

6 Bake the pie for about 20 minutes, or until the pastry has risen and is golden brown. Remove from the oven and allow the pie to cool for 10 minutes before eating.

SEA BASS

I have been fishing for many years. As a child I spent many hours either bracing the elements on Folkestone Pier after the elusive codling, or on the Hythe Canal (a 10-minute drive west of Folkestone) catching mostly eels and the occasional perch. It was good fun, and there was always that feeling of 'This will be my lucky day and I'll catch a monster.'

Once I left home I became more serious about fishing and took up fly-fishing. I really enjoyed pitting my wits against wild fish using an artificial fly. Not only was it much more exciting, but it meant I could travel with a small amount of gear, and almost stalk the fish. It also meant that I was constantly casting my line, and moving about, not just sitting there waiting for an unsuspecting fish to think, 'Hey, a juicy maggot, I'll jump on your hook.'

Bass fishing (not sea bass fishing, I was once told) follows many similar lines to trout fishing. They utilize the same criteria: use of an artificial lure; moving about all the time; and knowing where the fish are (the last point being slightly more difficult in the sea). But with bass fishing you also have to know at what time to go. I spent three long summers in Cornwall trying to catch the elusive bass. I tried everything – flies, lures, baits, sand eels, mackerel, squid, worms, the lot – to no avail. I went at dawn, morning, afternoon, evening, night. I went off the beach, the rocks, in a boat – you name it, I did it – but not once did I catch a fish, let alone a bass. It became a standing joke with the family and my wife even bought me a 'bass catching record book'. In it she wrote the headings '2001...no fish', '2002...no fish', '2003...no fish'. She took great delight in filling in the yearly catch record!

But one day that all changed. I met a guy called Damien who said he would take me bass fishing, and he did. On the way he explained to me that over the years so many bass have been caught – legally and illegally – that the stocks had considerably diminished. Damien had fished the area all his life, and the fish were now a lot smaller those he had caught before, although occasionally there was a decent-sized fish, over 1.3kg (3lb). He also said there was a minimum legal size that could be taken, even fishing off the beach or rocks. At the time, the minimum size was 32cm (13in) from nose to tail, and as from the 6th July 2007 it increased to 40cm (16in), due to the fact that so many immature fish are being caught these days.

That first trip out we didn't catch a thing, but a few days later and before I had even got my rod ready, Damien had caught a small bass, about 675g (1½lb). Lo and behold, a few minutes later I caught my first bass, again a small fish but nevertheless a bass. Quickly, Damien took a photograph as evidence for my wife. That was a couple of years ago, and since then I have had many good fish, but it's still all down to timing, place, and of course the fish being there in the first instance – and it is still as exciting.

Then, of course, from a chef's point of view, there is nothing better than catching a beautiful wild fish, preparing it, and then cooking it simply and correctly with the respect it deserves. For me, all the recipes here elicit the best flavour and texture possible from this so-called 'wolf of the sea'. Even my daughter Grace loves it.

BAKED SEA BASS WITH SWEET POTATOES AND RED WINE DRESSING

With a fish as beautiful as bass, I think that the less you do with it the better. I once went to a small restaurant in Hong Kong where you pick your fish from the tanks in the restaurant and they cook it while you wait. The fish was simply grilled and baked whole, and served with a hot dressing spread over it. It was really delicious, because it was so simple. So here is my version, also very simple, but a great dish to cook for a dinner party.

Serves: 4-6

1 x 1.6kg (3 ½lb) whole line-caught bass, scaled and gutted

olive oil

salt and freshly ground black pepper

Sweet potatoes

4-5 tbsp olive oil

a pinch or two of dried red chilli flakes

2 medium sweet potatoes, peeled and cut into 2cm (¾in) cubes

Dressing

1 small red onion, peeled and very finely chopped

3 tbsp red wine vinegar

3 tbsp Japanese rice wine

2 pinches caster sugar

6 tbsp extra virgin olive oil

4 tbsp chopped parsley

1 Place the olive oil for the sweet potatoes in a large wok and heat. Preheat the oven to 230°C/450°F/Gas 8.

2 Add the chilli flakes to the hot oil, then the sweet potatoes, and coat these well with the olive oil and chilli. Season well then turn the heat right down. Cover with a lid. (Most large saucepan lids will not fit into a wok, but don't worry too much, it just needs to cover the food. You can use foil if you prefer.) They will probably cook in 20 minutes.

3 While they are cooking, cut the fins off the bass with a pair of scissors, leaving the head on. With a sharp knife, neatly score the fish one way right down its length, just under the skin.

4 Place the fish in a large baking tray. Drizzle over a little olive oil and season well. Bake for about 20 minutes.

5 Meanwhile, place all the ingredients for the dressing, apart from the parsley, in a bowl, and season well. Add the parsley and mix well.

6 After about 20 minutes, check the potatoes: they should be soft. If cooked, remove from the stove and season again. Keep warm.

7 To test the bass is cooked, use two spoons to gently pull the flesh apart. The flakes should fall apart, with a little resistance, but not be overcooked. If the fish is not cooked, return it to the oven for 5-6 minutes. Once cooked, cover with foil and leave to rest for 10 minutes.

8 Spoon the sweet potatoes around the outside of the fish, then spoon over all the dressing. Take the whole tray to the table, and let everyone help themselves. The only addition I'd recommend is a crisp green salad, with plenty of cucumber, cress, watercress and spring onion, lightly dressed with lemon juice and olive oil.

PAN-FRIED SEA BASS WITH TOMATO SAUCE, NEW POTATOES AND RUNNER BEANS

Serves: 6

6 medium bass fillets, scaled

3 tbsp olive oil (extra virgin if possible)

juice of ½ lemon

675g (1½lb) new potatoes, Charlotte or Jersey Royal

2 small onions, peeled and finely chopped

2 garlic cloves, peeled and crushed

1 x 400g (14oz) can chopped tomatoes

1 tsp caster sugar

1 bunch basil, chopped

salt and freshly ground black pepper

800g (1¾lb) runner beans, topped and tailed

unsalted butter

Bass is my favourite summer fish. I've matched them here with tomato compote, an extremely full-flavoured tomato sauce, and runner beans, which I love. You can also buy baby farmed bass and cook them whole – great for the barbecue.

1 Place the bass fillets in a shallow dish or bowl and sprinkle over 1 tbsp olive oil and the lemon juice. Cover the dish with clingfilm and leave in the fridge for an hour.

2 Cook the potatoes in a pan of gently simmering salted water for about 15 minutes, or until tender. Drain well and keep warm.

3 Meanwhile, heat 1 tbsp olive oil in a pan. Add the onion and garlic and cook gently until softened and golden, about 10 minutes. Add the tomatoes, sugar, basil and some seasoning, then continue cooking gently for about 10-15 minutes, or until the liquid has evaporated and the mixture is fairly thick.

4 Remove the tough strings from the sides of the runner beans with a sharp peeler. Slice the beans into 7.5cm (3in) lengths, then cut into thin strips and cook in a pan of boiling salted water for about 5 minutes, or until just tender. Keep warm.

5 Heat the remaining 1 tbsp olive oil in a large frying pan. Remove the bass from the dish and pat dry with kitchen paper. Add to the pan, skin-side down, and fry for 4-5 minutes. Carefully turn the fish over and cook for a further 4 minutes, or until cooked.

6 Spoon a little of the tomato compote into the centre of warmed plates, and sit a bass fillet on top. Serve with the warm, buttered new potatoes and runner beans. Simple but great.

PAN-FRIED SEA BASS WITH 'SQUEAKY BEANS'

When I was in New Zealand once, a friend cooked me shark – he simply pan-fried it with a squeeze of fresh lime, over a campfire. It was one of the freshest pieces of fish I have ever eaten, and I will never forget it. I applied this idea to a bass I caught in Cornwall last year, and cooked it for myself late one evening. My daughter Grace asked if she could try it. She loved it, and I have since had to cook the dish many times. My other daughter Winnie also loved it, and she liked the thin Kenya beans I cooked and served with it. When you cook the beans slightly, they attain a 'squeaky' texture when chewed. This is not really a recipe, more of a simple process, with great results.

Serves: 4

1 x 2kg (4 ½lb) whole line-caught bass, gutted, scaled, filleted, and boned, but skin on, cut into 4 nice pieces
salt and freshly ground black pepper
2 tbsp plain flour
6 tbsp olive oil
juice of 2 large limes

To serve
225g (8oz) thin string beans, topped and tailed

1 Pat the fish dry with kitchen paper, then season well with salt and pepper. Dust with the flour.

2 Heat the olive oil in a frying pan, but don't get it too hot. Add the fillets, skin-side down, then cook for 4-5 minutes on each side. The secret is to very slightly undercook the fish. Add the juice of 1 lime and a little salt and pepper.

3 Meanwhile, cook the trimmed beans in plenty of boiling salty water for a few minutes only. Drain well.

4 Place a nice pile of green beans on a large plate. Top with the cooked bass and an extra squeeze of lime juice. Serve straightaway.

CLOTTED CREAM
A.E. RODDA'S

To get the measure of Cornish clotted cream you might as well start at the beginning. So it was that I found myself visiting dairy farmer John Brock at Trevilla Farm, near Truro. A softly-spoken Cornishman, John took me straight out to meet his herd of 80 cows. I thought he was pulling my leg when he told me he knew them all by name, but the cows had all been born on the farm that John's run for the past 39 years. They were virtually family.

Soon John's herd knew exactly what time it was and where to go, and ambled down to the dairy to be milked. Once in the parlour, John made me milk one of them by hand. Blimey, it was hard work, and I was grateful when he broke out the proper milking equipment. A short time later, the herd's rich unpasteurized milk was in a milk-tanker and so was I, up-front and ready for the journey to Rodda's clotted-cream plant near Redruth.

Less than 100 years ago the 75 acres that A. E. Rodda's creamery is built on was amongst the most valuable land in the world due to the copper and tin it contained. Today the mining has ended, but Rodda's sits on a veritable gold mine of its own. For Rodda's is the byword for clotted cream, the rich, thick cream-with-a-crust that is a true symbol of Cornwall but is exported all over the UK and beyond, to wherever a scone or apple pie is found to be underdressed.

Rodda's has been a family firm since its humble beginnings in a Cornish farm scullery in the late 19th century. These days it may be a vision of stainless steel, steam and white tiles, but it is still run by Eric Rodda, now in his late eighties. The day I visited, it was his nephew Alfred who showed me around.

The cream-making process is relatively simple. It's the grand scale that's truly impressive. Some 80 workers make 10 tons – 10 tons! – of cream a day. First of all, the milk and cream are separated in centrifuges. The thin milk goes off to become milk powder while the thick double cream is cooked in ovens, in the plastic pots that will eventually grace supermarket shelves. It's the cooking and cooling that give the distinctive crust. The thickest cream rises to the surface, boils, bubbles then forms a crust. In old Cornish dialect, this crust was called a 'clout', meaning a patch, which is where the name 'clotted' comes from: clouted cream.

Occasionally EU food laws work to our benefit and since 1998 no other county, let alone country, has been allowed to make 'Cornish clotted cream', even though the same stuff is made in Devon and, bizarrely, the Lebanon. Did the ancient sea-faring Lebanese traders, the Phoenicians, bring the recipe for clotted cream, or did they take it away with them, when they used to sail all the way to Cornwall to buy tin 3,000 years ago?

Somehow, having seen the whole process through, it seemed right to find myself on the Rodda family lawn with a huge plate of scones, some jam and of course a pot of their gooey cream. And I remember phoning my wife Fern to warn her we'd need a fair bit of space in the fridge that evening for the vat of cream that I'd come away with.

In these health-conscious times, it gladdens my heart – whatever else it may have done to it – to hear that Cornish clotted cream is going from strength to strength. Oh, and the Rodda family concern has never needed to spend a penny on advertising.

August - The butter fat content is slightly higher in summer, so we enjoyed thick, rich clotted cream on our scones

DARK CHOCOLATE AND CHERRY CHRISTMAS PUDDING

This recipe was developed by a friend and colleague of mine, Steven Poole. We wanted a twist on a normal Christmas pudding. So often these days you see and eat bitter, jet-black puddings that are packed down so firm you can't cut them. This pudding is lightly packed into the bowl and has a loose, open texture that crumbles slightly. Also, I've not used beef suet, just olive oil. It's a change from the norm, but we think a great result.

Serves: 8

40g (1½oz) each of sultanas, currants and raisins

40g (1½oz) dried figs, chopped

60g (2½oz) large glacé cherries, quartered

1 tbsp black treacle

4 tbsp extra virgin olive oil

1 small apple, cored, peeled then grated

2 tbsp whisky

40g (1½oz) plain flour

25g (1oz) molasses sugar

15g (½oz) cocoa powder

2 tsp mixed spice

1 tsp salt

85g (3oz) bitter chocolate, 70% cocoa solids, grated

1 large egg, beaten

1 x 227g (8oz) tub clotted cream, to serve

1 Mix together the dried fruit, treacle, olive oil, apple and whisky and leave for at least 4 hours, or overnight if possible.

2 Mix all the dry ingredients together.

3 Add the egg to the soaked fruit and mix well. Finally add the dry ingredients and mix well; do not over-mix.

4 Place the mixture in a pudding basin, 17cm (6½in) in diameter and 9cm (3½in) deep, and cover with a circle of greaseproof paper. Place a large piece of foil on top of a large piece of greaseproof paper, then fold in the centre to make a pleat. Place the pleated papers on top of the pudding basin and use a long piece of string to tightly tie the papers just below the rim of the basin. With an extra piece of string, tie a long loop across the top – you can use this as a handle to help lower and lift the pudding in and out of the pan.

5 Place a heatproof saucer in the bottom of a large saucepan and sit the pudding on top. Fill the pan with enough boiling water to come halfway up the sides of the basin, then cover with a tightly fitting lid. Bring the water to the boil, reduce the heat and simmer gently for 4-5 hours. Check the water every couple of hours and add extra boiling water as necessary to maintain the water level until the pudding is cooked. Serve with clotted cream.

STRAWBERRY AND HAZELNUT SHORTCAKE

The combination of English strawberries and hazelnuts works well. As an apprentice, one of the first jobs I had was to roast and skin hazelnuts. It's a real pain, but now, thankfully, you can buy roasted, skinned hazelnuts ready to go. Make sure you chill the shortbread completely before rolling it. It will make the job much easier, especially on a warm day. English strawberries are the best by far – pick up the punnet, and if you get a wonderful aroma of sweet strawberries, then 99 per cent of the time they will be perfect. If there's no aroma, don't buy! Wash the fruit before 'hulling' (removing the stalk); this prevents the strawberry filling with water and going soggy.

Serves: 4

500g (18oz) fresh strawberries

lemon juice, to taste

caster sugar, to taste

a touch of cold water

1 x 227g (8oz) tub clotted cream

unrefined golden icing sugar, for dusting

Shortbread

175g (6oz) cold unsalted butter, cut into small cubes

115g (4oz) caster sugar

225g (8oz) plain flour

175g (6oz) shelled hazelnuts, roasted and chopped

1 Place the cold butter and the sugar in a mixer and beat until soft and slightly creamy; do not over-beat. Add the flour and hazelnuts and mix to a firm dough. Wrap in clingfilm, press flat and chill well for about an hour.

2 Wash and then hull the strawberries, then lay them out on a plate. Pick out half of them, the nicest shaped ones, and reserve. Pop the others into a liquidizer and blitz with a little lemon juice, sugar and water until you have a nice thick sauce. I have purposely left the quantities out, as it's really up to your taste preference. Sieve the sauce through a fine sieve and adjust the taste (do not over-sweeten). Chill well.

3 Preheat the oven to 190°C/375°F/Gas 5.

4 Cut the shortbread dough into two pieces; place one back in the fridge. Gently knead the dough until it is slightly soft, then roll it out on a lightly floured work surface, to about 5mm (¼in) thick. Carefully cut out four large circles, about 8cm (3¼in) in diameter, using a pastry cutter (an inverted tea cup is also a good size).

5 Lift the shortbreads and place on a greased baking sheet. Bake until slightly brown, about 10 minutes. Repeat the process with the other piece of shortbread, so you end up with 8 cooked discs. Cool completely.

6 The next part in the simplest. Lay four shortbread discs on four plates. Arrange the whole strawberries on top (you may need to slice some), then spoon on a large dollop of clotted cream and a little strawberry sauce. Top with the other four discs of shortbread and heavily dust with unrefined icing sugar. Serve straightaway with extra strawberry sauce.

I love this pudding — it's quite dense and has a rich flavour. The milk chocolate and the hazelnuts combine really well and, coupled with the tartness of the stewed apples, make a great autumn/winter warmer. The clotted cream is of course optional, as is vanilla ice-cream, or both...

STEAMED HAZELNUT AND MILK CHOCOLATE SPONGE PUDDINGS WITH STEWED BRAMLEY APPLES

Serves: 6

150g (5½oz) unsalted butter, melted, plus extra for greasing

75g (2¾oz) shelled hazelnuts, roasted and chopped

100g (3½oz) milk chocolate, melted

4 medium eggs, at room temperature

125g (4½oz) caster sugar

140g (5oz) plain flour

Stewed apples

2 large Bramley apples

70g (2½oz) unrefined demerara sugar

a dash of water

juice and zest of 1 large unwaxed lemon

To serve

1 x 227g (8oz) tub clotted cream

85g (3oz) milk chocolate, melted

1 Place a steamer on the stove and half-fill with water. Bring to the boil, place the steamer tray in and cover with the lid. Butter six 9 x 6cm (3½ x 2½in) deep plastic pudding basins well, and butter six pieces of foil large enough to cover the tops of the basins.

2 Grind up the hazelnuts with a rolling pin so they are in small pieces; you don't want dust. Add to the warm melted butter along with the melted chocolate and mix well.

3 Place the eggs and sugar in a bowl and whisk until very thick and foamy. Carefully fold in the flour. Then fold in the melted butter, chocolate and nut mixture. Take your time and make sure it's all incorporated.

4 Carefully spoon the mixture into the greased pudding basins. Do not fill more than half-full, as the sponge will need to expand when it cooks. Cover with well-buttered foil and seal well, by scrunching the foil around the top of the mould. Place in the steamer and steam for 35-40 minutes.

5 Meanwhile, peel, core and chop the Bramleys into small pieces. Place in a saucepan with the demerara sugar, water and lemon juice and zest. Cook for 20 minutes, stirring occasionally, until you have a nice pulpy mixture, then keep warm.

6 Once the puddings are cooked, carefully remove from the steamer and turn out into warm bowls. Add a large spoon of apple compote to each plate and spoon on top a nice dollop of clotted cream and a little melted milk chocolate, and serve.

Creamy mousses usually need some sort of setting agent, gelatine being the most popular. Pectin and agar-agar are others that set well without the firmness of gelatine, but you can also use Italian meringue (great for ice-creams). Here, the reaction between the acid of the fruit and the cream and condensed milk makes a great setting. A word of warning though: this mousse will set in seconds, so work swiftly to get it from the bowl into the mould or dish. The cardamom in the shortbread works well with the sharpness of the lemon and lime.

CLOTTED CREAM AND LEMON CURD MOUSSE WITH CARDAMOM SHORTBREAD

Serves: 6-7

Mousse

finely grated zest and juice of 3 unwaxed lemons

finely grated zest and juice of 1 large unwaxed lime

1 x 300g (10½oz) tub full-fat soft cream cheese

1 x 397g (14oz) can condensed milk

1 x 227g (8oz) tub clotted cream

150g (5½oz) good-quality lemon curd

Shortbread

225g (8oz) plain flour

115g (4oz) cornflour

225g (8oz) unsalted butter, softened

55g (2oz) caster sugar

55g (2oz) icing sugar, sieved

8 green cardamom seeds, crushed and made into a fine powder

To serve

85g (3oz) bitter chocolate, 70% cocoa solids, melted

sherbet powder

1 To make the shortbread, sieve the flour and cornflour together. Beat the butter and sugars together in a bowl until soft and fluffy. Add the cardamom powder to the butter and sugar mixture along with the flour and cornflour, and then knead well to make a dough. Shape into a ball then flatten and wrap in clingfilm. Chill well, for about an hour.

2 Preheat the oven to 180°C/350°F/Gas 4. Grease two baking sheets.

3 Roll out the dough to about 5mm (¼in) thick, then use a 7cm (2¾in) diameter cutter to cut out the biscuits. Place on the baking sheets, and bake for about 12-15 minutes, or until pale golden brown. Allow to cool slightly on the baking sheets before transferring to a rack to cool completely.

4 To make the mousse, start off with the citrus juice. It is most important that the total amount of the lemon and lime juice is 250ml (9fl oz) or the mousse will not set well.

5 Whisk the cream cheese, condensed milk and clotted cream together until thick and very creamy. The longer you whisk, the lighter the mousse will be. Add the lemon curd, juices and zests and whip for a few seconds only, as the mixture will tighten very quickly. Immediately spoon into small dishes or a large trifle bowl, then chill until set, ideally overnight.

6 To serve, spoon the mousse into bowls or eat from individual dishes. Drizzle a little melted bitter chocolate over the shortbread and serve separately. Dust with sherbet powder.

BLUEBERRIES
TREHANE BLUEBERRIES

There's not much the Trehane family from Wimborne in Dorset doesn't know about blueberries. Jennifer and David are the third generation to grow these wonderful sloe-black berries. Grandfather David Trehane planted the first berry bushes in the UK after the Second World War, imported from their native home in North America and Canada. It was a gamble, but the first bushes to arrive thrived in our soil and climate, and their cultivation has carried on in this corner of Dorset ever since.

Today, the Trehanes harvest some 20 tons of blueberries every year from a scant five-acre site. The two dozen pickers the Trehanes employ can be busy from July right through September.

It's a pretty slick operation. The freshly picked fruit are sorted and weighed in their picking baskets. The plumpest berries are sent straight to the vast chilling room to limit the ripening as best they can until they hit the supermarkets' and greengrocers' shelves. Some go to farmers' markets while a few are requested by chefs for their restaurant kitchens. The smallest are reserved as cooking ingredients, where it doesn't matter what size they are so long as that wonderful sharp flavour shines through.

Taking heed of the pick-your-own sign, I was given a punnet and invited to try my luck, and I have to say it's harder than it looks. Although I might be able to fill a punnet in something approaching the 15 minutes achieved by old hands at this lark, my berries would not be in such pristine condition as theirs. Supermarket buyers are notoriously picky, and condition is everything.

Picking the blueberries is only half the battle. The Trehanes are fanatical growers too. As Jenny is quick to tell me, there's way more to cultivating blueberries than simply broad-casting fruit pips into the ground. The family have their own nursery where they nurture 15 different varieties of slow-growing blueberry micro-plants until such time as they are ready for planting out or selling on to other enthusiasts. Even devoted 'parent' Jenny admits the rearing of blueberries is a 'slow tedious process'.

Once they are fruiting, the battle is not entirely over. Blueberry bushes are quite labour-intensive to maintain for a healthy crop. They need regular trimming to force new growth and promote fruit development. Dorset is ideally suited to blueberry production because they love free-draining acidic soil. Other UK growers are situated in Norfolk and Suffolk, never far from the sea.

The Trehanes cultivate three main types of blueberries: high bushes, which can be up to about 2.7 metres (9 feet) tall, like the staple Duke variety; a couple of varieties of squat bush; and some hybrids which, if nothing else, save on all that reaching up or bending down.

I'm delighted to say that the men and women of science have finally caught up with Grandfather Trehane's intuition. Some 50 years on from the first planting in that lovely loamy Dorset soil, we are told that blueberries are a 'superfood' and wonderfully good for us. No fruit is as high in antioxidants as the blueberry. They are packed full of vitamins A, C and E, and wonderfully beneficial for circulation and eyesight. It's even thought blueberries may help protect against some cancers. Whatever their health value, I am delighted to say they are also a wonderfully tasty and versatile ingredient for chefs.

July - The height of the blueberry season, and we picked handfuls of fruit on a warm rainy day

PORK BRAISED WITH BLUEBERRIES

I use elderberries that I have dried myself. Eight heads will produce about 350g (12oz) fresh berries which, once dried, will reduce in volume by about half. To dry the berries, place them on a non-stick tray and place in a very cool oven, say 110°C/ 225°F/ Gas ¼. Dry for about 6-7 hours.

Serves: 4

4 tbsp vegetable oil

1 x 1kg (2½lb) hand of pork, skin and fat removed, then cut into 3cm (1¼in) pieces

3 tbsp plain flour

500ml (18fl oz) dry cider

1 pork or chicken stock cube, dissolved in approx. 300ml (10fl oz) water

2 tbsp caster sugar

1½ tbsp sweet smoked paprika

2 tbsp each dried elderberries and blueberries

1 large onion, peeled and very finely chopped

3 tbsp pearl barley

salt and freshly ground black pepper

200g (7oz) thick Greek yoghurt

6 tbsp chopped parsley

1 Preheat the oven to 180°C/350°F/Gas 4.

2 Heat the oil in a large casserole. Place the pork and flour in a bowl and mix together well. Place the pork into the hot oil and brown all over, then add the cider, and stock and mix well. Stir in the sugar, paprika, elderberries, blueberries, onion and barley. Season, mix well and just bring to the boil. Cover with a tight-fitting lid immediately.

3 Place in the oven and cook for 1¾ hours.

4 Remove from the oven and leave to stand for 20 minutes. Stir in the yoghurt and serve with plenty of chopped parsley.

BLUEBERRY AND CRÈME FRAÎCHE PORRIDGE

This is a twist on a great breakfast idea I had 15 years ago. Basically it uses up leftover porridge, and tastes great. Even my children will eat this. I think it's the soft texture of the porridge and the creaminess of the crème fraîche that's a hit. Blueberries always go down well with kids, so that's the easy part. But any fruit will work, especially semi-dried fruits at Christmas time; just soak them first in a little cold tea and fruit juice.

Serves: 4

140g (5oz) cooked cold porridge, no salt, broken up with a fork

4 tbsp runny honey

400g (14oz) crème fraîche

1 x 100g (3½oz) honeycomb, cut into 1cm (½in) pieces

juice and finely grated zest of 1 small lime

55g (2oz) unrefined golden caster sugar

350g (12oz) blueberries

1 Place the porridge in a bowl and mix with the honey and crème fraîche. In a separate bowl, place the honeycomb, lime juice, zest and caster sugar.

2 Gently crush some of the blueberries with a potato masher to break up the fruit very slightly. Carefully stir the blueberries and the honey mixture into the porridge, so you end up with a 'ripple' effect.

3 Spoon into wide glasses or a large bowl. Chill well.

FRESH BLUEBERRY MILLE FEUILLE

Serves: 4-6

1 x 375g (13oz) pack all-butter
ready-rolled puff pastry

2 tsp vanilla extract

6 tbsp unrefined icing sugar

300ml (10fl oz) double cream, very
lightly whipped

5 tbsp damson jam

300g (10½oz) blueberries

icing sugar, to dust

6 tbsp flaked almonds, lightly browned

The classic mille feuille is usually made with strawberries, but I reckon this could be better. The whole blueberries lend themselves very well to this type of dessert. Coupled with damson jam and cream, they make a great pudding: very simple to prepare, cook and serve. Remember not to over-whip the cream.

1 Preheat the oven to 200°C/400°F/Gas 6.

2 Place the puff pastry on a greased baking sheet. Prick well with a fork, and score one-third at the end with diamond shapes. Then put it in the hot oven and cook for 15-20 minutes, or until risen and golden brown. Take care with puff pastry: it burns very quickly once you take your eye off it. Remove from the oven and transfer to a cooling rack to cool.

3 In a bowl, stir together the vanilla, icing sugar and cream. Do not over-beat or the cream will split. Keep as cold as possible.

4 Cut the pastry into three equal pieces lengthways. Spread two of the layers with damson jam (don't skimp): not only does it sweeten the dessert, but it also brings out the flavour of the blueberries. Then place the blueberries on top of the jam on both layers. Using a palette knife, spread a thick layer of whipped double cream on top of the blueberries and jam. Carefully, using a palette knife again, lift one of these strips of pastry on to the top of the other and nestle down nicely. Put the final piece of puff pastry on top and, using the cooling rack, press down lightly. This is quite important because if you don't press, it will be extremely difficult to cut. Don't worry too much about excess cream coming out from the edge.

5 Take the palette knife again and, using any excess cream from the bowl and from the edge of the pastry, carefully fill in the gaps around the layers of pastry and blueberries. Once nice and tidy, dust the top heavily with icing sugar. Carefully stick the browned almonds to the outside edges of the pastry.

6 It's best to eat this dessert within an hour or the pastry will start to soften. The nicest thing about this dessert is the wonderful combination of textures and flavours. The easiest way to cut the slice is to use a serrated bread or carving knife in a sawing motion.

SWEET AND SOUR BLUEBERRY RELISH

As children, we spent a lot of the summer holidays just outside Blackpool picking whimberries (tiny native blueberries). My grandmother would turn them into the most scrummy pie and ice-cream. Different parts of the country have different names for this fruit. In Somerset, for instance, they are called whortleberries. My grandmother would sometimes cheat and use the dried variety, which are pretty good, and work well in all sorts of dishes. This relish is a smashing accompaniment to cold roast meats, roast game and even roast turkey.

Serves: 6

200ml (7fl oz) dry red wine

50ml (2fl oz) red wine vinegar

1 large onion, peeled and very finely chopped

1 tsp English mustard powder

1 tsp ground allspice

1 cinnamon stick, broken in two

¼ tsp red chilli powder

a pinch each of salt and freshly ground black pepper

1 x 340g (12oz) jar redcurrant jelly

750g (1lb 10oz) fresh blueberries

1 Gently bring to the boil the wine, vinegar, onion, mustard, allspice, cinnamon, chilli and salt and pepper, and simmer until reduced by half, which will take about 20 minutes.

2 Add the redcurrant jelly and blueberries and cook over a steady heat until thickened and pulpy, stirring all the time. This will probably take 30 minutes or so.

3 Cool and put in a sterilized jar. It will keep for a month in the fridge.

MUM'S BLUEBERRY DIGGLES

My father named these 'diggles' after the hole in the top of the raw mixture before it's cooked. Heaven knows where it came from, but it stuck well. My mum still makes them: they are delicious, soft and slightly chewy.

Makes: 12

85g (3oz) blueberries

1 tbsp granulated sugar

'Diggles'

85g (3oz) butter or margarine

225g (8oz) self-raising flour

85g (3oz) caster sugar

1 medium egg, beaten

1 Rinse the blueberries and stir in the sugar to coat them. Set aside.

2 Preheat the oven to 200°C/400°F/Gas 6.

3 Rub the butter or margarine into the flour in a bowl, add the caster sugar, and make a well in the centre. Add the egg to the well, then mix until you have formed a dough.

4 Break off 12 pieces from the dough, and shape into rough balls about the size of a large walnut. Place on to a sheet of silicone paper on your baking tray, leaving a good gap in between them. Make a decent-sized dent in the top with the end of a wooden spoon, then spoon in a few blueberries – about 4 should fit.

5 Bake for approximately 12 minutes. They will spread slightly and should be just golden. Remove and cool.

THE
SOUTH

WATERCRESS
CHARLES BARTER

Charles Barter's watercress operation at Manor Farm is situated in the heart of the Hampshire countryside at leafy Alresford. It came as no surprise to me to learn that Manor Farm has been in the same family for generations. Its layout looks quaint and historic. The sound of babbling water is soothing.

The Barters grow their cress in big but shallow beds strewn with gravel for the cress to curl its roots into. The beds are fed with endless quantities of fresh-running, circulating water – a million gallons every day. Not surprisingly Charles Barter has had his own boreholes sunk a hundred feet down into the chalky soil to guarantee an endless, drought-resistant supply of the clear stuff.

I was amazed to see that not only does the cress have its feet immersed in water but it gets a shower too, from non-stop sprinklers stretching across the beds. I was told this constant misting keeps the leaves perky on the hottest of English summer days but also stops insects landing on the plants, so the cress does not need dousing in costly, toxic pesticides.

Tim Jesty, farm manager and the fourth generation of his family to work in the cress business, took me into the propagation polytunnels where the watercress seeds are first sown. It's a very old-fashioned, labour-intensive process, scattering the seed by hand on to damp peat. It's pretty haphazard too, as only one in every 3,000 seeds will actually germinate – a pretty poor ratio by modern crop-husbandry standards. It is an indication, however, of what a natural, un-genetically modified and damned stubborn product cress actually is.

Still, once it germinates, cress grows like a mad thing. In the summer, it takes just a week for cress seeds to become 5mm (¼in) seedlings with a dense root-mat. This growth is scraped off the peat, the root-mat is literally torn into shreds to divide it, and it's taken to be planted. Sylv and Sandra, two veterans of the cress business, were waiting in a virginal gravel bed, and invited me to help them sow the adolescent cress. With 53 years' experience between them, they made short work of covering the vast bed with thrown shreds of cress and roots. The seedlings take just five weeks to develop into a lovely green crop that is ready for harvesting.

These days, tractors have replaced the horses that were used to get the cress as far as the pack-house, where in a din of conveyor belts and water jets the cress is washed, weighed and packed ready for the supermarket shelves.

Growing a crop is pointless if you can't get it to market still looking appetizing, and in the mid-19th-century, the cress business in Hampshire was so big and the demand elsewhere so high that Hampshire gained its own railway line. The Watercress Line, as it has become known, opened in 1865 purely to ferry cress up to London's Covent Garden market. The cress was taken to Alresford station each evening by horse and cart and it was on sale in the West End of London the next morning.

These days the cress has been replaced by 120,000 tourists a year, all carried in perfect safety by a team of enthusiastic volunteers who run the Watercress Line as if it were a gigantic train-set. I got some indication of what life must have been like in the cress business a century and a half ago when I was invited up into the cab with the crew to drive the train. My Dad – a model train buff – was so jealous!

WATERCRESS-STUFFED SEA TROUT WITH TARRAGON CREAM SAUCE

I think sea trout (or salmon trout) is by far the best of all the spring and summer fish. It has a wonderful delicate flavour and needs very little cooking, and even less in the way of sauces, flavourings and seasonings. Here, I've matched it with tarragon, watercress and flat mushrooms: all the flavours work well and are not fighting against each other. Sea trout's fine flavour must be due to the fact that, like wild salmon, it spends most of its life in the sea, only returning to a river to spawn (when they get caught, which is why you normally only see them in the shops from March until early summer). When I lived in the West Country, I became accustomed to using this beautifully flavoured fish in the summer. Most supermarkets now stock farmed sea trout in season, and very good they are too.

Serves: 2

1 x 1.3kg (3lb) sea trout, scaled and gutted

salt and freshly ground black pepper

25g (1oz) unsalted butter, melted

Stuffing

3 tbsp olive oil

3 small shallots, peeled and very finely chopped

1 garlic clove, peeled and very finely chopped

100g (3½oz) flat mushrooms, sliced

2 tsp lemon juice

1 medium egg yolk

55-85g (2-3oz) fresh breadcrumbs

½ bunch watercress, about 125g (4½oz), roughly chopped

Sauce

100ml (3½fl oz) Noilly Prat or similar vermouth

100ml (3½fl oz) cold water

a pinch or two of a fish stock cube

1 shallot, peeled and chopped

175ml (6fl oz) double cream

2 tbsp chopped tarragon

1 Preheat the oven to 220°C/425°F/Gas 7.

2 To make the stuffing, heat the olive oil, add the shallot and garlic, and cook over a low heat for about 3-4 minutes, until soft. Add the sliced mushrooms and cook for a further 10 minutes. You will probably find a little water cooks out of the mushrooms, but do not worry – cook until all the liquid has evaporated. Add the lemon juice and follow the same procedure. Remove from the heat and leave to cool. When cool, add the egg yolk, breadcrumbs, and about a third of the watercress and season well with salt and pepper. You need to end up with a firm, but not too firm, stuffing. The breadcrumbs will continue to soak up the juices once inside the trout, so leave the mixture slightly loose.

3 Place the sea trout on a chopping board. Place your index finger under the gills at the back of the head, and push your finger into the flesh, until you reach the spine. Next, carefully run your finger as close to the spine as possible, along the entire length of the fish. You will find the flesh will come away quite easily from the spine. Once you get to the tail, stop. Cut the head and tail off with a sharp knife, then pull out the bone. If you find a few bones left in the belly, remove them with tweezers or a small pair of pliers. (You could ask your fishmonger to do this for you.)

4 Season the fish well inside and out, then pack in the stuffing and re-shape the fish to roughly its original shape. Cut in half with a knife, using a light sawing action and taking care not to let the stuffing squidge out.

5 Grease a large, deep baking dish with the melted butter. Pop the two pieces of fish into the tray, add the Noilly Prat, water, fish stock and shallot. Cover tightly with foil and bring to the boil on the hob, then put in the oven for 12-15 minutes, or until the fish is opaque, and just cooked.

6 Carefully strain off the juices into a small saucepan. Bring the juices to the boil and reduce rapidly by half. Add the cream and bring back just to the boil. Season well and add the remaining watercress, stalks and all (lots of flavour is in the stalks), to the sauce, along with the tarragon.

7 Uncover the trout, then carefully remove the top skin with a sharp knife. It will come away very easily indeed, exposing the beautiful, pink, moist flesh.

8 Bring the sauce back to the boil, so the tarragon and watercress are just wilted. Serve the fish in deep bowls and spoon over the sauce. A few boiled new potatoes to serve it with are all you need.

MACKEREL ROLLS WITH WATERCRESS KETCHUP AND FLATBREADS

Serves: 4

4 medium mackerel fillets, boned but skins left on

salt and freshly ground black pepper

olive oil, for brushing

2 tbsp chopped basil

2 tbsp pitted black olive rings

Ketchup

3 tbsp olive oil

2 small onions, peeled and very finely chopped

1 garlic clove, peeled and very finely chopped

300ml (10fl oz) water

½ vegetable stock cube

2 tbsp light soy sauce

2 tbsp runny honey

1 level tbsp cornflour, slaked in 2 tbsp cold water

255g (9oz) watercress

3 heaped tbsp frozen peas

3 tbsp mayonnaise

a squeeze of lemon juice

Breads

225g (8oz) self-raising flour

2 tbsp good-quality olive oil

4 tbsp chopped mint

4 tbsp natural yoghurt

I had the idea for this bread from my good friend and Ready Steady Cook colleague, Lesley Waters, an excellent and very clever chef. Not only is it very quick and easy, but it makes a great accompaniment to all sorts of dips and sauces (and, rolled out even thinner than below, makes a good base for canapés or finger food).

1 To start the ketchup, heat the olive oil in a large saucepan, then add the onion and garlic and cook for 5 minutes to soften. Next add the water, stock cube, soy and honey, bring to the boil and cook for 5 minutes. Then thicken with the cornflour, stirring it in well.

2 Add 85g (3oz) of the watercress and all the peas, and cook for a further 1-2 minutes until the watercress is softened. Pour into a large tray or bowl over ice and water to cool as quickly as possible. This will keep the deep green colour.

3 Once cooled, spoon the cooled mixture into a liquidizer, add the remaining watercress and blitz for a good 3-4 minutes, or until very smooth. Whisk in the mayonnaise and lemon juice, and chill.

4 Meanwhile, for the breads, preheat a griddle or frying pan. Mix the self-raising flour, some salt, the oil, mint and yoghurt together to form a loose dough (using a little water if needed). Roll out to about 1cm (½in), or possibly slightly thinner; do not overwork.

5 Pop the breads straight on to the hot dry griddle or frying pan and cook on each side for about 4-5 minutes, or until slightly puffed and blistered. Leave to cool then and cut into wedges or strips.

6 Preheat the oven to 200°C/400°F/Gas 6, or the grill to a moderate to high heat.

7 Lay out the mackerel fillets on your work surface, season well with salt and pepper, and brush with olive oil. Sprinkle on a little chopped basil and a few rings of olive. Roll up and secure with a wooden cocktail stick. Brush with more oil.

8 Heat a non-stick, heatproof and ovenproof pan, and add a touch of oil.

9 Place the rolls into the pan and cook for 2-3 minutes. Place into the oven or under the grill for 10 minutes. Do not overcook. Serve the rolls with the breads and the watercress ketchup.

WATERCRESS AND NETTLE BREAD

Makes: 1 x 900g (2lb) loaf

450g (1lb) strong bread flour

1¼ tsp salt

2 tbsp extra virgin olive oil

1 x 7g sachet (1 tbsp) quick-acting dried yeast

300ml (10fl oz) warm water

1 tsp caster sugar

85g (3oz) fresh young nettle tops or leaves, roughly chopped

85g (3oz) watercress, roughly chopped

1 tbsp sherry vinegar

Nettles are not used that often these days, which is a shame because they have a unique flavour and are quite versatile. The golden rules when gathering nettles are: always use rubber gloves; pick the tips only; pick from hedges or gardens that have not been sprayed with weedkillers, and definitely not from roadsides; and finally, pick on a sunny day and then just rinse under cold water very briefly to keep their scent. Spinach can be swapped for nettles if you prefer.

1 Leave the flour in a warm place, overnight if possible. Then put the warm flour into a mixing bowl. Make a well in the centre, add the salt and olive oil and mix well.

2 Mix the yeast with half the warm water and all the caster sugar and add to the flour.

3 Add the nettles to the flour mixture, along with the watercress. Mix well and then add the vinegar and enough of the remaining warm water so that you end up with a soft dough. If your nettles and watercress are quite wet when they have been chopped, then you may need to add a little extra flour to tighten up the dough; just keep an eye on the mix.

4 Knead for a good 10 minutes. The dough should be free from stickiness and leave the edges of the bowl. Place the dough back in the bowl and cover with oiled clingfilm. Leave to rise in a warm place until the dough has doubled in size; this will take 30 minutes.

5 When the dough is ready, turn out on to a lightly floured surface. With a floured rolling pin, roll the dough to roughly 40 x 30cm (16 x 12in). Once rolled, roll up Swiss-roll style, place on a silicone-papered baking tray and slash the top in a criss-cross fashion. Dust generously with flour, cover with clingfilm and leave to prove until doubled in volume.

6 Preheat the oven to 220°C/425°F/Gas 7. Remove the clingfilm and place the bread into the preheated oven. Bake until the crust is nicely browned, about 30 minutes. Take the loaf out of the tin, place it back in the oven directly on the bars or on a small wire rack on a baking sheet, for another 5 minutes; this allows a crust to develop all around the loaf.

7 When the loaf is cooked, remove it from the oven and cool on a wire rack. Leave to cool completely before attempting to cut.

WATERCRESS FLATBREAD WITH HERBED EGGS AND BEETROOT

Serves: 4

300g (10½oz) self-raising flour

½ tsp salt

½ tsp freshly ground white pepper

6-7 tbsp extra virgin olive oil

approx. 150ml (5fl oz) cold water

100g (3½oz) or 1 small bunch watercress, roughly chopped

a pinch of chilli powder

1 large shallot, peeled and finely chopped

2 tbsp chopped coriander

2 pinches ground coriander

To cook and serve

olive oil, for brushing

4 medium eggs

salt and freshly ground black pepper

2 tbsp freshly chopped soft herbs (such as parsley, chives, basil, coriander)

8 pickled baby beetroots, drained

This unusual bread is based on naan, but made easier by using self-raising flour. It cooks quickly in a non-stick frying or griddle pan. The secret is to not let the pan get too hot or the dough will scorch. When I first cooked this bread my son was off school ill. He tried the bread and loved it. Bear in mind that this is a boy who can spot a speck of pepper at 200 yards and will steer clear of anything remotely green! It makes a great breakfast-brunch dish with fried eggs and pickled beets.

1 Mix the flour, salt, pepper and 4 tbsp of the olive oil together. Add the water, and knead to a softish dough; don't go mad. Cover and leave for 10 minutes.

2 In a bowl mix the watercress, chilli powder, shallot, fresh and ground coriander and the remaining olive oil.

3 Split the dough into two, then roll each piece out to form a 15-18cm (6-7in) circle.

4 Place half the watercress mixture into the centre of each rolled-out dough circle. Bring the edges together, squeeze together at the top, then flatten slightly. Roll flat with a rolling pin, until you see the watercress coming through. Leave to rest again, uncovered, for 10 minutes.

5 Heat a griddle pan or non-stick frying pan until fairly hot. Brush the flatbread with a little olive oil. Place the flatbread on or in the pan, and cook for 3-4 minutes. Flip over and cook for a further 3-4 minutes. Once cooked keep warm. Do the same with the second flatbread.

6 Fry the eggs in a little oil with plenty of salt and pepper until cooked to your taste, then sprinkle with the herbs.

7 Cut the flatbreads in half, and place an egg on top. Serve with the halved baby beets.

WATERCRESS, MUSSEL AND NEW POTATO TART

Serves: 4-6

1 x blind-baked shortcrust pastry flan or tart case, 24cm (9½in) in diameter and 4cm (1½in) deep (see page 17)

250ml (9fl oz) whipping cream

1 pinch fish stock cube

25g (1oz) unsalted butter

1 small onion, peeled and finely chopped

1 garlic clove, peeled and crushed

1 pinch saffron stamens or a pinch of good-quality saffron powder

1kg (2¼lb) mussels, cleaned, cooked and meat removed from the shell; you need about 300g/10½oz meat

1 bunch watercress, chopped, stalks and all

100g (3½oz) cooked new potatoes, peeled and cut into small cubes

2 tbsp chopped parsley

salt and freshly ground black pepper

2 medium eggs

2 medium egg yolks

Mussels are probably the cheapest shellfish you can buy, ranging from 75p to £1 per kg. They are a bit of a pain to clean and prepare but well worth the effort. Nowadays most mussels come rope-grown, which means they are in free-flowing water, thus suggesting no or very little grit or sand. Having said that, mussels can still be slightly gritty and sandy, so take care to check them over very carefully. Discard uncooked mussels any that are still open if you tap them lightly and any cooked mussels that fail to open. This tart is best served warm.

1 Preheat the oven to 180°C/350°F/Gas 4. Take care to cook the flan at this medium heat or the custard will split and curdle. Put the pastry case on a baking sheet.

2 Bring the cream to the boil, add the pinch of fish stock, and whisk until the stock has dissolved.

3 Melt the butter in a pan, add the onion, garlic and saffron, and cook to soften slightly. Spoon into the bottom of the pastry case, then top with the mussels, watercress and potatoes. Sprinkle over the parsley, and season well with salt and pepper.

4 Whisk the eggs and yolks together, and carefully pour on the warm cream. Whisk lightly to combine.

5 Strain the cream mixture into the flan case and pop the baking sheet into the oven. Cook until the flan is just set in the middle, about 25-30 minutes. The residual heat will finish the flan off if you leave it for 15 minutes to set.

6 When set and cooled slightly, cut and serve. I like to serve with a little blob of mayonnaise and a cucumber salad.

GARLIC
COLIN BOSWELL

It was a happy accident that saw the Isle of Wight become synonymous with lovely fat heads of English-grown garlic. Colin Boswell's mum planted some cloves in her farmhouse kitchen-garden during the long hot summer of 1976, and they did so well Colin is planting and harvesting garlic bulbs on an industrial scale some 30 years on.

Mersley Farm is in the Isle of Wight's picturesque Arreton valley and it is ideally suited to growing the famous 'stinking rose'. It has the well-drained soil garlic likes, not too acidic. In the winter, Colin can rely on a nip of frost to coax the garlic into growing plenty of bulbs, spring rain to swell the cloves, then lashings of the island's famous sunshine to dry the bulbs out in summer. There is actually little art to growing healthy heads of garlic. Yet Colin, his wife Jenny and their three children have turned his mum's experiment into such a thriving business I just had to cross the Solent to see what he was up to.

Traditionally, any time-served gardener will tell you to 'plant on the shortest day and harvest on the longest' – i.e. plant December 21st and harvest on June 21st – but I was interested to discover that Mersley Farm plants its garlic from October through to February, while harvesting runs for two months from June.

Colin first started growing a garlic variety from the Massif Central but these days he kick-starts his year with the lovely early pink crop known as Early Wights then moves on to Purple Wights with their bigger bulbs and later growing, before the main Solent Wights that a French person would recognize as 'Auvergne'.

I visited Mersley Farm in high summer and was delighted to see just what a traditional process garlic harvesting is. The bulbs are eased out of the ground by hand. Many of the Boswells' seasonal workers come back year after year and actually relish the back-breaking work. After the lovely creamy bulbs are lifted, they go into the Boswells' greenhouses to be baked by the sun. Proper drying is an essential part of the process as it delays the cloves from sprouting green shoots in the autumn, effectively rendering them useless in the kitchen. Another important treatment to preserve garlic is refraining from cutting off the long green stem that appears above the soil. Leaving it intact and allowing it to wither prevents shocking the bulbs and also gives the pickers something to plait or 'grappe' – a posh word for tying a cluster of bulbs into a posy. There's something delightfully 'country-kitchen' about a professionally presented bunch of garlic, especially when it's home-grown like this.

I'm never without as good-quality garlic as I can get in my kitchen. Its beautiful bouquet is essential to so many dishes from almost every continent on earth. Cooks have been using it for thousands of years to add flavour and healthfulness. It's said the pyramid-building slaves were fuelled on garlic, their masters being aware of garlic's health-giving properties even if they didn't know exactly why. Today, science tells us that garlic is packed with potassium, vitamins B and C, calcium and protein. It is said to clean the blood and fight various cancers as well as possess antiseptic, antibacterial and antifungal properties. What a fantastic foodstuff!

I'm pleased to say Colin has become a local hero on both sides of the English Channel he lives so close to. Mersley Farm stepped into the breach this year as the French saw their pink garlic harvest fail due to rising temperatures, leaving them desperately short of their famous cooking ingredient. For the first time, in a classic coals-to-Newcastle story, Colin and his family found themselves busy supplying French supermarkets with English-grown garlic. Anyone who can sell garlic to the French has to be doing something right!

TOMATO AND SMOKED GARLIC SAUCE

I like the simplicity of this sauce, and it's so easy to cook. The flavour and colour become more intense the more you cook the sauce. I like to stew chicken thighs in this sauce, and I also braise monkfish or salmon. It's so versatile, and even reduced down to a dip/spread consistency, with a little added oil, makes good eating.

Serves: 4

4 tbsp olive oil

1 large onion, peeled and finely chopped

4 smoked garlic cloves, peeled and chopped

1 tsp dried marjoram

1 tsp dried oregano

175ml (6fl oz) dry white wine

2 tbsp tomato purée

1 x 400g (14oz) can chopped tomatoes in juice

4 tbsp red wine vinegar

1 vegetable stock cube

1 tbsp caster sugar

salt and freshly ground black pepper

1 Heat the oil, add the onion, garlic and dried herbs, and cook gently for 10 minutes to soften. Add the wine and tomato purée; cook for a further 10 minutes. Finally, add the tomatoes with their juice, the vinegar, stock cube, sugar and some salt and pepper, and cook down slowly for 10 minutes until thick and pulpy.

2 Serve hot over pasta, with grilled meats or fish, or cold as a bread topping with a few black olives sliced through. A little freshly grated Parmesan cheese stirred through makes a nice change.

ROAST ELEPHANT GARLIC TOASTS

There really is no secret here, just well-roasted garlic. Strangely, the bigger the garlic gets, the less powerful its flavour becomes. Colin Boswell's elephant garlic is superb for roasting, and its sweet mellow flavour works well for this dish.

Serves: 4-6

2 large elephant garlic heads

4 tbsp olive oil

salt and freshly ground black pepper

6 thick-cut slices sourdough bread

unsalted butter

1 Preheat the oven to 220°C/425°F/Gas 7. Slice the bottom off the garlic heads, about 2cm (¾in) to reveal the open cloves.

2 Heat an ovenproof frying pan with the olive oil. Once hot, season the cut bottom of the garlic with salt and pepper, then place cut-side down into the hot oil. Place the pan into the oven and cook for 35-40 minutes.

3 Meanwhile, toast the sourdough slices and keep warm.

4 Check the garlic is cooked. It should be very soft and mushy and really well coloured.

5 Squeeze the garlic cloves out on to the toast and spread evenly. Dot with a little unsalted butter and more salt and pepper, then serve.

AVOCADO AND BUTTER BEAN GUACAMOLE

Serves: 4

1 x 410g (14oz) can butter beans, drained

1 small shallot, peeled and roughly chopped

2 garlic cloves, peeled and crushed

1-2 tsp sherry vinegar

about 1-2 tbsp cold water

1-2 tbsp extra virgin olive oil

1 ripe avocado, peeled and flesh raked out with a fork

2 small ripe tomatoes, finely chopped

juice of 1 large lime

2 tbsp chopped coriander

salt and freshly ground black pepper

Everybody has their own version of guacamole, and this is mine, mixed with canned butter beans. I like to use the canned ones because they really are delicious and a lot less time-consuming than having to soak overnight then boil for hours on end. The butter beans give a nice body to the dish. Not only is this a good dip to eat in front of the telly with a large glass of white wine, it also is a great summer lunch dish accompanied by grilled meat and fish. For instance, it's nice to simply grill a salmon steak with a little butter or olive oil and plenty of salt and pepper for a few minutes on each side (do not overcook), then serve with a spoonful of the guacamole and a few minted new potatoes.

1 Put the beans, shallot, garlic, vinegar and water into a food processor and blend until smooth. You may need to add a touch more water so you have a firm but not solid consistency. Then add enough oil to let down the mixture so that it's smooth and gloopy.

2 Remove from the food processor, add the avocado, tomato, lime juice and coriander and mix well. You want to retain a slightly rough texture. Taste, then adjust the seasoning if necessary with salt and pepper and possibly a squeeze more lime juice. You may also need to add a little olive oil.

3 Eat at room temperature with breadsticks, crackers, tortillas or even poppadums.

PAN-FRIED MONKFISH WITH RED WINE AND GARLIC SAUCE

Serves: 2

8 large garlic cloves

salt and freshly ground black pepper

25g (1oz) unsalted butter

1 tbsp olive oil

2 x 225g (8oz) large monkfish fillets

Sauce

350ml (12fl oz) red wine (Shiraz is perfect)

4 level tsp unrefined white sugar

250ml (9fl oz) strong fish stock

a little fish stock cube

2 pinches five-spice powder

25g (1oz) unsalted butter, cubed

1 tbsp double cream (optional)

The sauce for this dish is used more as a seasoning, and you only need very little to complement the delicate bass. A hint of five-spice and a touch of sugar just balance the strong red wine flavour perfectly. The sauce can be made well in advance, warmed and finished at the last moment. I like to have a little cooked tagliolini and a few spoons of sautéed leeks with the fish, and the sauce spooned over.

1 Trim the roots off the garlic cloves carefully. Do not peel. Cook the cloves in simmering salted water for 10 minutes, until very soft, then drain. Keep to one side.

2 For the sauce, place the wine, sugar, stock, stock cube, a pinch of salt, and the five-spice powder into a stainless-steel or ceramic pan. Bring to the boil and then gently simmer for about 10 minutes, until you end up with roughly a quarter of the original volume. Add the cold butter, whisking it in gently, and reduce until you have exactly 75ml (2½fl oz) left. The sauce will now have thickened nicely and have a wonderful gloss and shine. Add the cream if you want to at this point. Season again, cover and keep warm.

3 Heat half the unsalted butter and the oil in a frying pan until just foaming.

4 Season the monkfish fillets well with salt and pepper, add to the pan, and cook for about 4 minutes on each side. Turn off the heat, cover loosely with foil and leave to rest for a further 5 minutes, until cooked.

5 In a separate frying pan, gently sauté the cooked garlic cloves (skin on) in the remaining butter until golden.

THE
SOUTH-EAST

FLOUR
SARRE MILL

There's something very pleasing to the eye about a windmill in the landscape. Although a set of giant sails in the distance is a relatively common sight on the Norfolk Broads, where they are used as much for pumping water as for grinding grain, windmills are rare in Kent, where I grew up. In fact, Sarre Mill, near Canterbury, is now the only commercial windmill left in my county – a lovely piece of clean, green, industrial heritage.

It's little short of a miracle that this Kentish mill exists at all, because it closed at the end of the Second World War and lay derelict for some 40 years until it was bought and renovated as a labour of love. The huge sandstone mill-wheels began turning once again in 1985; they are turned by wind power when conditions suit, and at other times by a discreet electric motor. I was slightly disappointed to discover this until I was told the mill had had steam-powered assistance as far back as 1820 and gas power in 1945. Under the present enthusiastic ownership of local Liz Bligh, the mill earns its keep all year round, the electric motor ensuring flour can be produced to meet demand whatever the wind is doing.

Sarre is a so-called 'smock' mill. The body is planted firmly in the ground, while the top part, the 'cap' carrying the sails, can pivot through 360 degrees. A so-called 'fan-tail', on the opposite end of the cap to the sails, catches the wind and automatically turns the whole cap and sails to the optimum position to constantly catch the wind. What a lovely piece of equipment! So simple, yet so efficient.

On the day of my visit I hooked up with miller Derek Adams to help grind part of the mill's daily 1½-ton haul. There's nothing much to it, as a windmill is a marvel of nature-assisted simplicity. The wheat comes to Sarre from a local farm. The huge sacks are unloaded, garrotted with a chain and then hauled in through the door of the mill and up into the cap using the mill's own winch. During the Second World War, the mill was actually operated by German prisoners-of-war, and their signatures can still be seen on the beams and typically Kentish weather-boarding.

Up there in the confined space, I helped Derek wrestle with the heavy sacks and pour the lovely golden grains into a huge hopper. Gravity takes care of the rest. The grains flow down a chute and in between the French-made stones. Sarre Mill actually has two sets of mill-wheels with a mechanism to switch the sail-powered drive-shaft between them. One pair of millstones can be used for 'soft' wheat grains that are hardly to be found these days, the others – the French Burr stones we were using then – are much coarser and cope far better with the bullet-hard grains of Kentish wheat Liz buys in.

With a nod to me that the process was about to begin, Derek offered up the cog to the mill-wheel gears to begin grinding the wheat. He has a handle which offers fine adjustment of the stones' running to give coarse or fine flour. A hatch below the grindstones allows Derek to check on the flour itself. The whole process is regulated by eye, hand and nose. Experience and a sniff of the powdered wheat tells him whether the grindstones are getting too hot and the flour is burning or not.

The end-product is sieved. The process separates out the finest white flour from the coarser wholemeal flour. The really rough stuff goes back to the farm as cattle-feed. Nothing is wasted.

January – milling flour on a freezing day was incredibly hard work

TREACLE AND PRUNE FLOWERPOT BREAD

I like to cook bread in flowerpots but the trouble is you have to find the old-style, hand-thrown pots; the newer ones seem to crack when you cook at high temperatures. I found mine in a junk shop whilst I was waiting for the ferry back to the mainland from the Isle of Wight. This treacle and prune bread works well with all cheeses, spread thickly with unsalted butter. Lightly toasted, it's a nice base for beans on toast topped with a few crispy rashers of dry-cure bacon or a grilled Cumberland sausage. The bread freezes well so there is no excuse for not trying it – you won't be disappointed

Makes: 4 flowerpot loaves

700g (1lb 9oz) malted granary flour

2 x 7g (¼oz) sachets easy-blend dried yeast

75g (2⅔oz) unsalted butter, melted

3 tsp salt

2 tsp caster sugar

150g (5¼oz) semi-dried prunes, roughly chopped

200ml (7fl oz) bottled spring water, lukewarm

200ml (7fl oz) full-fat milk, lukewarm

1 large tbsp black treacle

To finish

1 medium egg, beaten

3-4 tsp black onion seeds or poppy seeds

1 Place the flour, yeast, melted butter, salt, sugar and chopped prunes into a mixing bowl and mix well.

2 Add equal amounts of water and milk and the treacle, and mix until you have a soft dough. You may not need all the liquids so take care and only add about three-quarters of each at first.

3 Knead well on a lightly floured work surface for 5 minutes. Place back in the bowl, cover with clingfilm and leave to rise in a warm place for 30 minutes, or until doubled in size.

4 Preheat the oven to 220°C/425°F/Gas 7. Line four 14 x 12cm (5½ x 4½in) ceramic flowerpots with baking parchment.

5 Remove the dough from the bowl and lightly knead. Do not over-work or it will be difficult to roll out. Cut the dough in four equal pieces, about 400g (14oz) each. Roll each into a ball, then pull slightly to one side, into almost a teardrop shape, to ensure they fit into the bottom of the flowerpot. Place into the lined flowerpots and cover with clingfilm. Leave to prove for 30 minutes or until the dough is just touching the top of the pots.

6 Carefully remove the clingfilm and lightly brush the tops with beaten egg then sprinkle with poppy seeds.

7 Bake in the oven for 30-35 minutes or until well risen and golden.

8 Remove from the oven, turn the loaves out of the pots, and place back on the baking tray and into the oven. Bake until the sides and bottom are golden, about 10 more minutes. When cooked, cool on a wire rack.

BUTTERMILK, HONEY AND CARAWAY ROLLS

Makes: 30 rolls

25g (1oz) easy-blend dried yeast

500ml (18fl oz) buttermilk, warmed

750g (1lb 10oz) strong white bread flour

1 tsp bicarbonate of soda

1 tsp cream of tartar

3 level tsp salt

4 tbsp runny honey

55g (2oz) caraway seeds

100ml (3½fl oz) full-fat milk, warmed

75g (2¾oz) unsalted butter, melted

Baking bread has been a large part of my professional career. It's very therapeutic. I was once told by a good baker that the longer it takes to prove and make bread, the better the end result. I mostly agree with this, but sometimes we have had to make bread in a rush and so have only let it rise once – you can still get good results. What makes a difference is the quality of the flour: flour with a high gluten content will make perfect bread. I quite like to use fresh yeast, but I also use the dried varieties, and, to be honest, I can't taste the difference. The choice is yours.

1 Place the yeast, half the warmed buttermilk and two handfuls of the flour into a large bowl and stir until you have a smooth batter. Cover with clingfilm and leave to rise for about 15 minutes in a warm place. This is known as 'the ferment'.

2 In a separate bowl, place the bicarb, cream of tartar, salt, honey, seeds and the rest of the flour, and mix well. Leave in a warm place.

3 When the ferment is light and frothy, mix with the dry ingredients, the warmed full-fat milk and melted butter. Add a little more warmed buttermilk, and mix to a silky but firm dough.

4 Mix and knead well for 5 minutes. Once well kneaded, return to the bowl, cover and leave to rise for a further 15-20 minutes, or until doubled in size.

5 At this point preheat the oven to 230°C/450°F/Gas 8.

6 Once the dough has risen, remove to a floured surface and knead slightly. Do not overwork. Cut the dough into two, then roll it into two sausages. Cut these into 55g (2oz) lumps, then roll each one into the size and shape of an index finger, or slightly fatter.

7 Place the rolls on a lightly oiled baking sheet. Dust with a little extra flour, then slash three times with a sharp knife or razor blade on the diagonal. Loosely cover again, and leave to prove until nearly doubled in size, about 45 minutes.

8 Unwrap the rolls and bake for 12-15 minutes. They will colour slightly and look puffed and light. Remove and cool. These rolls freeze well, both raw and cooked, although they will be slightly drier, with a crumblier texture.

EASY CIABATTA

Makes: 3 loaves

Sponge starter

5g (⅛oz) easy-blend dried yeast

165g (5¾oz) plain flour

165g (5¾oz) strong white bread flour

300ml (10fl oz) bottled spring water, warmed

Dough

1 x 7g sachet easy-blend dried yeast

250g (9oz) organic strong white bread flour

450g (1lb) plain white flour

15g (½oz) salt

10g (¼oz) milk powder

20ml (¾fl oz) olive oil

550ml (19fl oz) warm water

cornmeal, to thicken

I spent a long time trying to perfect a decent recipe, trying all sorts of flours, waters and oven temperatures. This is the best I made, and I reckon it's down to the mixture of normal flour, by that I mean everyday plain flour, and higher gluten bread flour. The dough has to be very, very soft, almost a dropping consistency – this makes a huge difference to the end-product. The classic, holey texture of this 'slipper bread' comes from a lack of working the dough.

1 Mix the sponge starter ingredients well together, cover and leave in the fridge for a minimum of 12 hours, best 24 hours, to ferment. Generally the dough should weigh about 500g (18oz) after 24 hours.

2 For the dough, place all the ingredients into a mixer, along with the sponge starter, and bring together well for at least 7 minutes. The dough should come away from the sides of the bowl but stick to the bottom.

3 Remove the dough from the bowl and continue to knead by hand on a lightly floured work surface for a further 2-3 minutes. The dough should be very elastic and velvety, and still sticky, to create the open texture. Cover and leave to rise until doubled in size, about 30 minutes.

4 Once risen, dust the dough well with flour. Carefully turn the dough out of the bowl on to a well-floured work surface. Do not knead the dough, just gently tease it into shape – you need to keep as much air in it as possible. Cut into three and gently stretch each piece of dough into an oblong shape, about 25 x 15cm (10 x 6in), then fold each piece of dough as though you were folding up a business letter. Dust heavily with flour, cover with a tea-towel, and leave to prove for about 20 minutes.

5 Preheat the oven to its maximum setting – about 230°C/450°F/Gas 8.

6 Once proved, carefully place the loaves on a baking sheet dusted with cornmeal. Using your fingers, push through the dough, leaving dimples all over it.

7 Bake for 15-20 minutes, or until well risen and golden. I like to spray the inside of the oven three or four times with a plant-pot water mister, which helps the crust develop and gives a nice colour and texture. Remove from the oven and cool completely on a wire rack.

SWEETCORN PIKELETS WITH CREAMY LEEKS

Serves: 4

2 medium corn cobs

10 tbsp olive oil

½ small onion, peeled and roughly chopped

4 medium eggs, separated

225g (8oz) self-raising flour

250ml (9fl oz) milk

a pinch of cream of tartar

6 tbsp roughly chopped coriander leaves

salt and freshly ground black pepper

2 large leeks, washed well, trimmed, cleaned and finely chopped

To serve

crème fraîche

wholegrain mustard

chopped coriander leaves

These little puffed pancakes, made with self-raising flour, are a real treat. They are simple to make and very tasty. All sorts of flavours can be added and they are a great accompaniment to most dishes. The raw mix will keep for a day in the fridge, but after that it loses its oomph!

1 Place one of the corn cobs on a chopping board, on its end. Carefully shave off the sweetcorn kernels all round with a sharp knife. Repeat with the second cob.

2 Heat 3 tbsp of the olive oil in a large frying pan or wok. Add the corn and sauté in the hot oil for 2-3 minutes, until it caramelizes slightly and takes on a nice colour. Tip on to a plate. Add a further 3 tbsp olive oil to the pan and repeat the process with the onion. Once cooked, spoon it on to the plate and leave it all to cool down.

3 Mix the egg yolks and half the flour together, then gradually whisk in the milk. Once smooth, add the rest of the flour and whisk until you have a smooth batter.

4 Whisk the egg whites with the cream of tartar until thick and foamy, then carefully fold into the egg yolk mixture, with the coriander, onion and sweetcorn kernels. Season well with salt and pepper.

5 Heat 2 tbsp of the remaining oil in a non-stick frying pan, then add large spoonfuls of the mixture – scoop the mixture up from the bottom of the bowl so you get some of the sweetcorn in each spoonful. Cook for 3-4 minutes, then flip over and cook for a further 2-3 minutes until well puffed and slightly browned. Repeat the process until all the mixture is cooked. Keep warm.

6 Meanwhile, heat the remaining oil in a wok or frying pan. Add the finely chopped leeks and stir-fry for 2-3 minutes, or until wilted slightly. Do not overcook. Season well, then strain into a colander and keep warm.

7 To serve, place two pikelets on each warm plate and spoon over the leek mixture. Top with a little crème fraîche, a tsp of wholegrain mustard and a little chopped coriander.

OYSTERS
WHITSTABLE OYSTER COMPANY

Going to Whitstable on the North Kent coast felt like something of a homecoming. It was a visit tinged with nostalgia, as I used to go there with my family when I was a child. Dad and I would go out hunting for winkles, cockles and other shellfish at low tide. Boiled for what seemed like an eternity, they'd be persuaded out of their shells with darning needles and eaten with vinegar. Even as a child I found them delicious. Today, though, I was in pursuit of shellfish of a much grander kind, and at low tide on Whitstable's shoreline evidence of their presence was all around, crunching underfoot.

Top-notch oysters are what Whitstable has always been about, and for London-based day-trippers, the quaint town has become a place of pilgrimage for lovers of these mysterious dollops of sea-fresh marine life, best eaten at a gallop and swallowed in one gulp.

There are four companies in Whitstable that own the oyster-fishing rights from the shore out for several miles, one of which was established when the ink was still wet on the Magna Carta. Locally, the companies' rule is absolute.

Boat-owner Andy Riches, who works for one oyster company, offered to take me out on his boat *Misty* on, admittedly, a less calm day than I'd have liked. Up until the 1950s, oysters were considered a poor man's food but a combination of rough winters and unchecked pollution conspired to kill so many that availability dwindled, the Kentish oyster fishermen went off hunting other cash-crops, and so the price went up for those few still being landed. They are so prized that it is well worth Andy's time and effort in all weathers.

We headed some four to five miles out past the oyster companies' beds to the shallow 'free' waters of the Kentish Flats in pursuit of the wild Whitstable native oysters. Harvest time for Andy is September to April, while over the summer months he dredges inshore for the Pacific rock oysters he personally introduced into these waters some five years back.

Although dredging may not sound the most eco-friendly means of fishing, Andy is gentle with the sea-bed – there is no other way of fishing for oysters short of diving for them. These days, sustainable fishing is uppermost in Whitstable's few remaining fishermen's minds. Oysters weighing in at less than about 8g (¼oz) go back overboard to mature. Baby oysters that have attached themselves to larger shells are carefully prised off and thrown back in.

On landing, the oysters are scrubbed clean and stored in huge salt-water tanks belonging to Richard Green of the Whitstable Oyster Company. He'd laid out a display of the best shellfish the Kent coast had to offer, both the Whitstable natives and Andy's Pacific oysters, which can grow to the size of a shoe if left to their own devices. As I was quick to point out to Richard, you can't learn much by simply looking at oysters, so with the aid of a sharp, stub-bladed knife, we got stuck in.

There is a knack to opening oysters. Using a tea-towel to grip the wet shell and protect your hand, you stick the stubby blade in the joint and work it along to cut through the muscle. Oysters do not yield their concealed treasure lightly, but they are well worth the effort. There is a definite difference between the local and imported oysters. While the Pacific oysters are good, they are markedly less fleshy and smooth tasting than the Whitstable oysters. It's no wonder local restaurateurs charge more for the native variety.

I know oysters are not to everyone's tastes but that sensual milky taste is like some kind of distillate of sea. There's nothing quite like it and Whitstable's oysters are among the very best in the world.

April - we went to sea for a couple of hours and couldn't resist tasting the oysters while on the boat; it's risky but well worth it

I'm a great believer in 'the less you play around with a beautiful ingredient the better'. I have never eaten, or cooked for that matter, a hot oyster dish that has the same flavour impact and intensity of the raw mollusc. I really cannot see the point in deep-frying, or grilling to hell and back, such a wonderful thing. The only other way of preparing them is to set them, raw, in a light jelly, sharpened with a little Chablis or Sauvignon Blanc and their own juice. This recipe balances the need for the deep-flavoured, iodine oyster kick, with the warmth of an autumn broth, without losing the freshness of flavour. I have cooked this soup for the best part of 20 years, and it's very simple. 'Cappuccino of' (I hate that term), the buzzword for frothy soups, or frothy anything for that matter (I have even had 'cappuccino of oxtail' recently, can you believe?), it does resemble, but that is unintentional. It's just a liquidized soup, which thickens naturally when the oysters are blended with hot cream and fish stock. This is why there is only one recipe in this section. I would advise you just to eat oysters raw, with a little lemon juice and black pepper. I even steer clear of the classic accompaniment of shallots steeped in vinegar; oysters are just too wonderful to muck about with.

OYSTER, SMOKED HADDOCK AND CHIVE BROTH

Serves: 4

200ml (7fl oz) strong fish stock

200g (7oz) natural smoked haddock

12 native or Pacific oysters, opened, including juice

freshly ground black pepper

6 tbsp finely chopped chives

600ml (1 pint) whipping cream

1 Heat the fish stock until it is boiling, then add the smoked haddock. Simmer for 1 minute, then remove the pan from the stove, cover with clingfilm and leave for 15 minutes. This gets the flavour of the smoked fish into the stock.

2 Meanwhile, place all the oyster flesh and juice into the liquidizer with a touch of black pepper.

3 After 15 minutes, remove the haddock from the pan and break up into four small, warm soup bowls. Sprinkle the chives evenly on to the fish.

4 Bring the whipping cream to the boil in a separate pan. Re-boil the smoked haddock-infused fish stock and add to the boiling cream.

5 Start the liquidizer and blitz the oysters for 15 seconds, then, whilst still liquidizing, carefully, pour in the boiling cream and fish stock mixture through the lid. Once all the liquid is in, leave for 1 minute.

6 Straightaway, pour into the four warmed bowls equally, and serve.

BEER
SHEPHERD NEAME

Growing up in Kent, I count the discovery of nut-brown hoppy beer as one of my formative taste experiences. The Shepherd Neame brand of real ales is a byword amongst brewers and beer fans alike. The Neame family's lovely red-brick premises has been sited on the banks of the creek in Faversham since 1698. Monks were brewing beer in the town as long ago as the 12th century. The Neames have a mere five generations' brewing experience under their belts. Today the brewing process is overseen by director Ian Dixon, who volunteered to show me round the plant.

My tour started off in an oast-house formerly used by Shepherd Neame. These distinctive red-brick towers were once where hops were spread out on a slatted drying floor over a hot air source. Related, believe it or not, to the cannabis family, hops add bitterness, flavour and aroma to your pint of real ale. These days the oast-houses are mostly silent, the drying being done in gas-fired kilns. Kent is still the number one hop-growing area in the UK, and Ian showed me how their hops arrive by dropping a compressed brick of greenery into my hands; it was waxy and laden with the unmistakable pungent smell of beer to come.

It's not just the hops that are treated to make beer. The main ingredient besides water is barley. To be usable in beer, the barley is put through the ancient process of 'malting', which means it's wetted, allowed to sprout, then roasted according to how dark a bitter is being made. This malting process unlocks the carbohydrates needed to make alcohol.

Back in the heart of the Faversham brewery, Ian showed me the two lovely old teak mash-tuns, installed during the First World War, which represent the start of the brewing process proper. Boiling water is added to the malted barley to create a porridge-like 'mash'. Through the steam, you could see giant paddles churning the mixture to unlock all the flavour. Run in tandem as they always are, there's enough capacity to make 50,000 pints of beer at a time.

The liquid, the 'wort' as it's called, is pumped out, checked for clarity through an ingenious porthole in the pipe-work and then goes into stainless-steel vats. Nothing goes to waste: the spent barley left behind in the mash-tuns is given to local Kentish farmers as cattle feed; the waste yeast from later on is fed to local pigs. In time, the pork and beef is bought and ends up on the menu in Shepherd Neame's pubs. Brilliant. As is Shepherd Neame's policy of buying bicycles for its local employees to cut down on traffic. I digress...

Ian next showed me the huge stainless-steel vats – giant kettles really – in which the wort is heated to 100ºC to sterilize it. Only then are those hops I've already seen added to the mix, which is cooled to blood temperature and pumped into huge fermentation vessels. At this stage Shepherd Neame adds its own various strains of yeast to kick off fermentation and modify the nascent beer's flavour in different ways. The brewery uses five different yeasts according to the beer it's making. That's about it, really.

I did get to see the bottling and barrelling plants, but what really interested me was the Bishop's room, where a team of lucky men and women are paid to try the beer. Where beer-tasting differs from wine-tasting is that you don't spit beer out. In beer-tasting, you need the brew to run over the base of the tongue and down the throat to assess its all-important bitterness, one of the last of beer's complex flavours to emerge.

BEEF SIMMERED IN BEER
WITH FLAT MUSHROOMS

Serves: 2

350g (12oz) good chuck steak, cut into 2cm (¾in) pieces, a little extra fat is fine

1 beef stock cube

300ml (10fl oz) water

300ml (10fl oz) Late Red Shepherd Neame beer or other winter ale

1 large carrot, peeled and chopped into 1cm (½in) pieces

1 small onion, peeled and finely chopped

a couple of pinches of caster sugar

salt and freshly ground black pepper

2 tbsp good-quality tomato purée

olive oil

4 large flat mushrooms

1 tbsp plain flour

40g (1½oz) unsalted butter, softened

This is a good autumn dish and it's so easy to cook. Just simmer and thicken, and there's no need to worry about oven temperatures or sealing the meat.

1 Place the beef, stock cube, water, beer, carrot, onion, sugar, salt, pepper and tomato purée into a saucepan and bring to the boil. Turn the heat down and barely simmer, partly covered, for 2–2½ hours. Keep checking the meat and do not overcook it or it will be dry and stringy. You may need to occasionally top up the liquid with a little extra boiling water to keep the meat covered.

2 Meanwhile, preheat the grill to its highest setting. Brush olive oil over the mushrooms and season well with salt and pepper. Grill for 15 minutes to dry out the mushrooms – once cooked they take on an almost meaty texture. Cut into 5mm (¼in) slices and reserve.

3 Mix the flour and softened butter together. Once the meat is tender, and the stock has reduced somewhat, stir in the flour and butter paste, and the stew will thicken nicely. If it ends up too thick, add a little water. Once thickened, stir in the cooked mushrooms and warm through.

4 Serve with plenty of mashed potatoes and a few roasted parsnips.

The whole point of a real barbecue is long, slow cooking. I cooked this recipe on a Weber gas barbecue; you can cook it on a charcoal barbecue, but you will need the kettle variety. With the gas variety, turn on the barbecue, then put the lid down. Heat the front burner only, until you get to 150°C/300°F, no hotter. At this point, place the meat into foil or a baking tray at the rear of the barbecue, so it is not over the heat. Put the lid down and leave it, apart from the occasional basting, for 4 hours. The temperature must be maintained at 150°C/300°F, minimum, and 160°C/325°F maximum. With a charcoal grill, light about 3kg (6½lb) charcoal in a chimney starter (a tube of metal: you stuff paper in the bottom and pack the top with charcoal). Light the bottom and in 10 minutes you have perfect charcoal to cook with. Tip this into the two side baskets and cover with the lid. Leave to get to the right temperature (see above) and adjust the heat using the vent on the top. Keep an eye on the temperature. After about 2 hours, light a second chimney of charcoal and top up the baskets when ready; this should be enough heat for the last 2 hours. You will get used to it – it just takes a bit of practice.

Makes: 2 rolls, to serve about 8

2 x 1kg (2¼lb) lean belly pork rolls, skin removed and tied well (your butcher will do this for you)

Rub

1 tbsp sweet paprika

3 tsp soft light brown sugar

1 tsp chilli powder

1 tsp celery salt

1 tsp garlic salt

1 tsp English mustard powder

1 tsp ground black pepper

½ tsp sea salt

Beer wash

30g (1¼oz) maple syrup

500ml (18fl oz) Spitfire Shepherd Neame or other summer ale

5g (⅛oz) garlic powder (a better flavour for this sort of cooking)

60g (2¼oz) dark brown sugar

a good pinch of dried red chilli flakes

1 tsp freshly ground black pepper

BARBECUED PORK 'BEER BELLY' ROLLS

1 Make up the rub and mix well. Pat over the pork rolls and place them into a foil or baking tray. The rub will just about cover the meat perfectly. If you can leave it for an hour or two, all the better; best of all is to leave it overnight.

2 Preheat the barbecue to 150°C/300°F. Place the tray with the pork to the rear of the grill, away from the front heat. Close the lid and cook for 4 hours altogether, but basting every 30 minutes.

3 Combine all the ingredients for the wash and get your brush ready. At the 30-minute mark, brush the joints with the beer wash, and continue to do so every 30 minutes for the duration of the cooking.

4 After 3¾ hours, check the internal temperature of the meat: it should be close to 160°C/325°F. If not, cook until it reaches that heat minimum.

5 Once cooked, remove from the barbecue, cover with clingfilm and leave to rest for 30 minutes before eating. This will ensure the meat will be tasty and succulent. It will be slightly underdone, but is perfect like this.

EARLY BIRD MUTTON, PARSLEY AND CAPER PLATE PIE

Young chefs are always taught to cook stews in the oven. This is basically correct, but I have found the cheaper, less well-known cuts of meat can be simmered with very good results. This dish is an example of how simmered meat can make a wonderful pie. The inclusion of mint sauce may raise a few eyebrows, but it works well. I recommend using Early Bird, Shepherd Neame's spring beer, which is light and hoppy and lends a great depth of flavour to this pie.

Serves: 6-8

2 x 30 x 24cm (12 x 9½in) discs ready-rolled shortcrust pastry

1 medium egg, lightly beaten

Filling

750g (1lb 10oz) boned shoulder of mutton, hogget or lamb, cut into 2cm (¾in) cubes, trimmed of excess fat

1 x 284ml bottle Early Bird Shepherd Neame or other summer ale

approx. 150ml (5fl oz) water

1 chicken stock cube

1 large onion, peeled and finely chopped

2 medium carrots, peeled and finely chopped

4 tsp mint sauce

25g (1oz) unsalted butter

25g (1oz) plain flour

2 tbsp capers, rinsed and drained

4 tbsp chopped parsley

salt and freshly ground black pepper

1 Place the mutton or lamb, beer, water, stock cube, onion, carrot and mint sauce into a saucepan and bring to the boil. Turn down to a gentle simmer and cook for 2 hours, maximum, with a lid half covering the pan. The slower the better.

2 Meanwhile mix the butter and flour together to form a soft paste (this is known as 'beurre manié').

3 Check the meat; it should be meltingly tender, and the liquid should just cover the meat. Spoon off any excess fat – there will be a small amount – then remove and discard about 6-8 tbsp of liquid. Bring the heat up under the meat to a gentle boil, and gradually add the flour and butter mixture in small pieces. Stir all the time and the gravy will thicken nicely. Do not burn. (If you want to cut down the amount of fat in this dish, then omit the butter; instead, make a soft paste with water and flour, and stir in in the same way as above.)

4 Once cooked, add the capers and parsley, then check the seasoning, and adjust if needed. Cool and chill.

5 Preheat the oven to 200°C/400°F/Gas 6.

6 Roll out the pastry slightly, as I think even though it is ready-rolled it can still be a little too thick. Use to line a non-stick plate pie tin about 24cm (9½in) in diameter, and about 4cm (1½in) deep. Spoon in the chilled meat mix and spread out slightly.

7 Roll out the other disc of pastry slightly. Brush beaten egg over the rim of the pie and carefully place the second disc of pastry on top. Press down the edges and neatly trim off any excess. Brush all over the pie with plenty of beaten egg, then make two small incisions in the middle.

8 Place on a baking sheet, and bake for 35-40 minutes, or until well browned. Serve with peas and mashed potatoes.

LAGER-STEAMED SALMON WITH BASIL AND LEMON

Serves: 6

6 x 140g (5oz) salmon fillet portions, skin on

salt and freshly ground black pepper

8 basil leaves

1 lemon, cut into 4 large wedges

200ml (7fl oz) sharp dry lager

This recipe sounds a bit weird, I know, but it really does work. I first cooked this on a beach in Jersey, whilst filming for This Morning, for a load of surfers, and it went down really well. The secret is to use a sharp, dry lager: Japanese Asahi is perfect. You can cook this over hot barbecue coals, or in a hot oven. I used special barbecue bags that have a clear plastic window in the top. This is not only to see if the food is cooked, but once it is, the clear plastic can be removed easily to get the food out. (These bags can be bought online from www.countrytrader.co.uk.) You can of course, just seal the salmon in two layers of foil, keeping the ends raised to stop the lager leaking out

1 If you are using a charcoal barbecue, light it well in advance and leave until the coals are grey. If you are using a gas barbecue, light to a high heat. If using an oven, preheat to 220°C/425°F/Gas 7.

2 Pack the salmon fillets into the bag or foil, skin-side down. Season well with salt and pepper. Add the basil leaves, lemon wedges and lager.

3 Seal well and place the packet on to the barbecue or into the oven. Cook for 10-12 minutes, do not overcook. The salmon should be slightly undercooked. Remember, the fish will continue to cook once removed from the heat source, so slightly undercook.

4 Serve straight from the packet, with tomato salad and warm new potatoes.

JAM
WILKIN & SONS JAM

Wilkin and Sons must be the biggest employer for miles around the Essex village of Tiptree. Some 200 people and up to three generations have worked at their factory or in their 1,000 acres of orchards and fruit plantations since Arthur Wilkin and a couple of friends set up the jam-making company in 1885. Although the family had been growing fruit in Essex for some 100 years, Arthur was only tempted into the preserves business by the poor prices he was being paid for his seasonal fruit at market. From small beginnings, Wilkin's jam has ripened into a company that now supplies 60 countries, and many of the airlines that fly to them.

Part of the secret of Wilkin's success is their insistence on just using sugar, pectin here and there to help the set, and the odd skilled application of citric acid or sodium citrate to help balance the acidity of certain fruits, nothing else. No preservatives, no colourings, nothing. The company may be coy about how much they produce, but they are clearly proud of the quality.

A visit to the quaint village of Tiptree is an excellent day out in the summer months. A stone's throw from the coast, the Wilkin family maintain a tea-shop and a small but fascinating museum. Their new farm manager positively welcomes visitors to tramp round his fields and orchards on a network of new public pathways, shaded by a mass planting programme of native trees. Land has also been set aside for nature reserves to help maintain the natural balance of insects and predators. In the summer months it is a paradise of heavy-cropping fruit bushes and traditional fruit trees as far as the eye can see.

Apart from obviously imported exotica like Seville oranges and pineapples, Wilkin and Sons either grow all the fruit they need or source it as locally as possible. I love visiting the factory and surroundings to see nature's bounty at its best: strawberries, greengages, plums, loganberries, mulberries, a new commitment to growing raspberries and even, at the end of the season, that wonderful old English fruit, the medlar.

Ducking indoors out of the sun, there is not actually much to the production line. It surprises many first-time visitors to see that even today Wilkin merely scale up what you or I would use in the kitchen to make our own preserves. There are copper boiling pans because stainless steel taints the fruit taste, while the cooking is done in small batches so as not to squash the fruit. Then it's into jars for setting, labelling and cooling and that's about it. All very recognizable and 'real', and all the better for it.

There aren't many companies left who produce foodstuffs just as they did 130 years ago, on an international, industrial scale, and yet can still make them taste as if they'd come fresh from a Women's Institute market stall. Wonderful.

SCONES WITH JAM AND CLOTTED CREAM

Makes: 10 x 7cm (2¾in) scones

250g (9oz) plain flour

200g (7oz) strong white flour

a pinch of salt

70g (2½oz) unsalted butter, softened

55g (2oz) baking powder

70g (2½oz) caster sugar

55g (2oz) milk powder

slightly over 300ml (10fl oz) cold water

milk or beaten egg, to glaze

To serve

clotted cream

greengage (or mulberry) jam

I was always taught to put sultanas or raisins into scones. But over the years I have had many complaints from customers telling me that fruit just does not go into scones. Well, it's a matter of choice, I think. It's very difficult to make scones consistently good, there are so many variables: flour strength, egg or no egg, butter or marge, milk or water etc. To me this is the best recipe. I actually got a version of it from a baker called Andy when we were filming in Broadstairs in Kent; you end up with a light, not dry, close-textured result. And of course there is much debate about how you load up your scone. Cream first or jam first? I prefer jam, then cream, but it's up to you; just make sure you load them well.

1 Preheat the oven to 220°C/425°F/Gas 7.

2 In a large bowl, rub the flours, salt, butter, baking powder, sugar and milk powder together. Make a well in the centre, and gradually add the water; the mixture should be quite wet. Remove from the bowl on to a floured surface and bring together to form a dough.

3 Roll out to a thickness of 2cm (¾in) and then cut out 10 x 7cm (2¾in) round scones. Place on a greased baking tray, and brush with milk or beaten egg.

4 Bake for about 15 minutes, or until well risen and light brown. Cool on a wire rack.

5 Once cooled, slice in half, thickly spread with clotted cream, then top with greengage (or mulberry) jam.

STEAMED MULBERRY JAM SPONGE PUDDINGS

Makes: 6 x 9 x 6cm (3½ x 2½in) puddings

100g (3½oz) salted butter, melted, plus extra for the moulds

9 tbsp mulberry jam

3 large eggs, at room temperature

finely grated zest of 1 unwaxed orange

125g (4½oz) caster sugar

100g (3½oz) plain flour, sieved

The mulberry was once called the 'king of British fruits' and I can see why. My first encounter with this delicious fruit was when I was in the West Country, and a doctor friend brought in 12 huge punnets of fresh mulberries, all picked by hand from his own tree (using surgical gloves as they stain skin very quickly), because mulberry trees can be huge. His was about 150 years old and was fully laden year on year. The berries were delicious and I just served them with thick clotted cream and a little unrefined icing sugar. Occasionally we would bottle them in sugar syrup for the Christmas menus, or make jam if we had a glut. This we would use in January for a delicious sponge recipe (as here) or in a baked or steamed jam roll.

1 Place the steamer pan on the stove and half-fill with water. Bring to the boil, then add the steamer tray and tight-fitting lid.

2 Butter the six 9 x 6cm (3½ x 2½in) moulds well, then place the jam evenly into the bottom of them.

3 Meanwhile whisk on high speed the eggs, orange zest and sugar until very thick and mousse-like. Remove the bowl from the machine and 'rain' over the flour using a sieve. Carefully fold this into the egg mixture. Pay particular attention to the bottom of the bowl, as the flour seems to miss being mixed here. I find it's best to fold it in with your hands, letting the mixture fall between them. This incorporates the flour perfectly without losing the lightness you have just whisked in.

4 When the flour has nearly been incorporated, add the butter, and again carefully fold together. It might look like the butter is not going to fold in, but it will. Take care, making sure to get to the bottom of the bowl. Pour or spoon the mixture into the moulds, just over half full. Cover with small squares of well-buttered foil. Pop into the boiling steamer, place the lid on, then steam for 30 minutes. Keep an eye on the boiling water: you may need to top it up with water from the kettle. I have found, though, that half a steamer full should be sufficient for 30-45 minutes' steaming. Once cooked, the moulds will be full and have a slightly domed top. Carefully remove from the steamer and leave for 5 minutes to set.

5 Remove the foil and turn the puddings out, domed-side down, into warm cereal bowls. Serve with plenty of hot custard.

STRAWBERRY AND WHITE CHOCOLATE CHEESECAKE

Serves: 8-10

175g (6oz) digestive biscuits, crushed

75g (2¾oz) white chocolate, melted

1 x 405g (14oz) can light condensed milk

2 x 250g (9oz) tubs mascarpone cheese

150ml (5fl oz) lemon juice
(4-5 lemons)

6 tbsp strawberry jam

To decorate

55g (2oz) white chocolate, melted

fresh strawberry halves, to decorate

Cheesecakes have always been a favourite of mine ever since my mother made a packet variety in the early 1970s. I love the combination of textures, and you can try so many flavours. Normally a cheesecake base uses digestive biscuits, mixed with melted butter in various quantities. Here I use melted white chocolate as the binding agent, which works perfectly.

1 Grease and base-line a 20cm (8in) springform cake tin. For the base, mix together the crushed biscuits and melted white chocolate, and lightly press into the tin. Chill for 2 hours minimum.

2 Meanwhile, beat together the condensed milk and mascarpone cheese until smooth. Add the lemon juice and combine thoroughly. Stir 3 tbsp of the jam, carefully, through the cheesecake mix.

3 Spread half the cream mixture on to the biscuit base. Spoon a little more strawberry jam on to the cream, then top with the remaining cream mixture. Chill for at least 4 hours.

4 Decorate the top of the cheesecake with fresh strawberries and a little melted white chocolate.

STEAMED LOGANBERRY JAM ROLL

Serves: 6

225g (8oz) self-raising flour

a pinch of salt

115g (4oz) suet

55g (2oz) caster sugar

1 medium egg, lightly beaten

approx. 2 tbsp cold water

185g (6½oz) loganberry jam

unsalted butter, for greasing

Steamed suet roll is one of the greatest winter puddings. When prepared and cooked correctly, it's a joy; when it's not, it's the worst pudding in the world. Use plenty of jam – the more the better; there is nothing worse than a mean jam roll.

1 Have ready a 24cm (9½in) steamer filled with boiling water. This is very important, for as soon as the pastry is ready it must be cooked, otherwise you will end up with a heavy, leaden pudding.

2 Place the flour, salt, suet, sugar and egg in a mixing bowl and mix well. Add a touch of cold water and mix to a soft but not sticky dough. Roll out straightaway until it measures about 30 x 40cm (12 x 16in).

3 Spread over the jam nice and thickly. Roll up lightly, then cut in half to make two manageable rolls. Tear off two pieces of foil roughly the size of the original pastry. Butter well, then place the rolls on top. Roll around the pastry loosely, then twist up the ends. Repeat with the second roll.

4 Place the two foil packages in the steamer and steam until the rolls are tight and firm, about 40 minutes. To test, gently squeeze – they should be full and firm. If not, then leave for a few more minutes.

5 Once cooked, carefully remove from the steamer, and leave the rolls to set. Open the foil and slice each roll into three. Serve with hot custard.

THE MIDLANDS

STILTON
CROPWELL BISHOP

Stilton is known to its fans as the 'King of English cheeses'. Here in the UK, pilgrims on the Stilton trail will inevitably end up in one of just three counties. Stilton cheese can only be so-called if it is made in Nottinghamshire, Derbyshire or Leicestershire, as it has been since the early 18th century. The Cropwell Bishop creamery I headed for is just south of Nottingham. Manager Andy Robinson was to show me the whole Stilton-making process.

It all begins in huge stainless-steel vats where the milk is pasteurized and supplemented with rennet to help it solidify. At this early stage a starter culture is added for flavour. Similar to penicillin and imported from Italy, the spores are stirred through the liquid – these will form the distinguishing blue streaks. As we watched the milk solidify into curds, Andy explained that the milk can vary between winter and summer, whether the cattle are indoors or out, being fed on cattle-cake or Nottinghamshire grass. All this can affect the finished Stilton if it's not handled correctly. Needless to say, Andy proved quite coy on their exact production techniques.

What is clear is that once the renneted milk has solidified to a blancmangey texture it is shredded into curds and salted for flavour and preservation. The loose curds go into tubular moulds and the waste water – the whey – is allowed to run off. These embryonic truckles of Stilton are turned end over end for 12 days in the 'hastening' room to shed moisture. I had a go and they are really heavy to manhandle.

Next was the interesting sounding 'rubbing-up room' where, after being rested overnight, the cheeses are firm enough to be removed from their moulds. At this stage, you can clearly see how 'loose' the texture of the curds still is, so workers go over each cheese with broad palette knives to smear the exterior, partly for appearance and also to prevent cracking. It's incredibly labour-intensive, but the mould grows from the heart of the Stilton outwards, and if the cheese were left alone without this drying and smearing it would literally blow apart. On day 35, the cheese is pierced to the core to get oxygen to the mould. Back

into storage and the truckles begin to form their characteristic crust on the outside, before any signs of the mould have made it out from the heart of the cheese.

It was at this stage of the Stilton's evolution that I was introduced to Howard, Cropwell's official taster. His job is to inspect and sample the Stilton, assess, then grade it for sale. Cheese-making – especially with introduced mould – is a black art, and the skill comes in achieving consistency between batches. Armed with a special corer, Howard took me into the storage area to find me some cheese to taste. To demonstrate how important careful maturation is, he gave me some eight-week-old Stilton, then the 'full-term' eleven-week-old cheese. The difference was incredible. The young cheese was really harsh, with the veining yet to reach the crust, while the mature cheese was buttery with a lovely open texture and some sweetness on the tongue.

They say, 'Drink a pot of ale and eat a scoop of Stilton every day and you'll live to a ripe old age.' It's a lesson the Japanese and Americans are learning, with Stilton exports rising every year. It's something Cropwell Bishop and indeed the whole Stilton industry should be proud of.

July - we tested the cheeses for ripeness with
an iron. A ripe stilton has a golden colour,
the cheese is creamy and the veining perfect

This recipe is simple, yet incredibly moreish. The idea of a cheese soup really did not appeal to me, but when I went to Italy a few years ago, I had a Gorgonzola and monkfish soup in Venice and it was superb, light and packed full of flavour. So, with that in mind, I played around with three great British staples and came up with this. You can vary the amount of Stilton used. I like a strong Stilton flavour, so I add more, but it's up to you. You should end up with a brilliant green soup that is not too thick. Watercress is possibly the only green vegetable that actually deepens in colour when cooked, provided it's not for too long and it's cooled quickly once cooked.

STILTON, WATERCRESS AND BRAMLEY APPLE SOUP

Serves: 4

2 medium onions, peeled and finely chopped
1 large Bramley apple, peeled, cored and finely chopped
1 litre (1¾ pints) vegetable or chicken stock
350-400g (12-14oz) Stilton, crumbled
200g (7oz) watercress
salt and freshly ground black pepper

1 Place the onion, apple and stock into a saucepan and bring to the boil. Turn down the heat and simmer for 20 minutes, or until the onions are very soft.

2 Add the crumbled Stilton and whisk in well. Simmer for a further 15 minutes, until the cheese has dissolved. Take care as the casein from the cheese will stick to the pan.

3 Bring the soup to the boil, then plunge the watercress into it and wilt for 2 minutes, stirring all the time.

4 Immediately and carefully, ladle a proportion of the soup into the liquidizer and blitz until smooth. Pour into a bowl and repeat the process, then season with salt and pepper. Cool quickly to keep the brilliant green colour.

5 When you want to eat, warm quickly and serve with crusty bread.

STILTON, WATERCRESS AND HONEYED PEAR WRAPS

Serves: 4

2 handfuls watercress, roughly chopped

200g (7oz) Stilton, crumbled

2 spring onions, sliced diagonally

freshly ground white pepper

2 tbsp olive oil

2 tbsp runny honey

4 large deli wraps

Honeyed pears

2 large Conference pears, halved, core and stalk removed

4 tbsp runny honey

2 tsp olive oil

The combination of these ingredients works really well. Most recipes call for a larger pear such as Williams Bon Chretien or Comice, but I really like Conference pears. This way, baked with honey, skin on, and seasoned with salt, pepper and olive oil, they are an absolute joy. Incidentally, this pear was named in the late 1800s when it was first tasted at a national fruit conference. It was well received, but nobody could agree on a name, so they called it Conference after, yep, the conference.

1 Preheat the oven to 220°C/425°F/Gas 7.

2 Place the pears in a dish or pan and drizzle over the honey and olive oil. Bake until soft and nicely browned, about 20 minutes, and allow to cool. Meanwhile place the watercress, Stilton and spring onion into a large bowl.

3 Slice the cooked pears into thin strips. Add to the cheese and watercress. Season with pepper, olive oil and honey and mix well.

4 Fold the wraps around the pear and Stilton.

STILTON WITH SWEET PICKLED QUINCES

Any preserved fruit works well with cheese, and it's nice to preserve fruit yourself if you have the time. I find the best way to cook quinces is to simmer them gently in sugar syrup until they are very tender. They can be quite deceptive: to test most fruits when poaching, you insert a skewer or knife into the fruit and there will be little or no resistance, but quinces have a very hard middle that does not soften with prolonged cooking. The only way to get rid of that is to cut it out once cooked. Quinces are great for jams and jellies. They give an extra kick to apple and pear crumbles: a little piece grated and added to the apple and pear chunks when raw can change the dish immensely. I like to make a very perfumed, powerful sorbet or even a flavouring for vodka with them. They can be poached, wrapped in clingfilm and frozen for later on in the year. I also like to add two or three raw and whole to the fruit bowl to give the whole room a wonderful sweet perfumed smell. The quince is one of the all-time-great English fruits (although brought here by the Romans). Most of the fruits these days are imported from Italy, Spain, Turkey and Iran, but you can find home-grown quinces all over Britain. It's still a very cheap fruit and one of my favourites. The flavours of blue cheese and quince work well together.

Fills: 1 x 750ml (1 ¼ pint) jar

Pickling time: minimum 1 month

2 large ripe quinces, 700g (1 lb 9oz) total weight

450ml (16fl oz) cold water

450g (1lb) granulated sugar

juice of 1 large lime

Pickle

75ml (2½fl oz) white wine vinegar

75ml (2½fl oz) perry vinegar (pear vinegar)

10 black peppercorns

150ml (5fl oz) quince-cooking syrup

75g (2¾oz) caster sugar

To serve

stilton

1 Place the quinces into a stainless-steel pan, along with the water, sugar and lime juice. The quinces must be covered with the sugar and water mixture. Bring to the boil, cover and simmer very gently until the fruit is soft. This can take as little as 45 minutes or as long as 1¼ hours, depending on the size and ripeness of the fruits. To test, use a skewer and pierce the fruit, there will be a little resistance due to the core of the fruit, which will not be softened by cooking. The rest of the fruit will be soft and succulent. Remove from the stove and cool with the lid on.

2 For the pickle, bring all the ingredients to the boil in a non-reactive pan and leave to cool.

3 Drain the quinces well, cut into quarters and remove the core. Carefully peel off the skin (or it can be left on if you prefer). Cut each quarter into small, uniform 2cm (¾in) chunks, and pack into a sterilized Kilner jar. Pour over the hot syrup until the quince is covered. Seal well, and leave for 1 month in a cool, dark place.

4 Serve with a large wedge of Cropwell Bishop Stilton and biscuits or bread – great on Boxing Day evening.

If you like Stilton, you will love this. In the days before the good old fridge, a lot of food was potted for eating at a later date. This process meant that food was cooked, roughly puréed, then spiced with nutmeg, saffron and mace, and mixed with an equal amount of fat, normally butter. It was then packed into stone jars and sealed with pure fat. This preserved the foods for long periods. These days, potting has gone out of fashion, probably due to its high fat content, but a good potted meat, game, fish or cheese is delicious. They have played a big part on my menus over the years, and will continue to do so.

POTTED STILTON WITH ROAST COX'S APPLES

Serves: 4

325g (11½oz) unsalted butter

2 small onions, peeled and finely chopped

2 garlic cloves, peeled and crushed

500g (18oz) Stilton, at room temperature

1 tsp English mustard powder

½ tsp hot chilli powder

1 tsp fennel seeds, finely crushed or ground

4 tbsp chopped parsley

125ml (4fl oz) Somerset cider brandy

2 tsp Worcestershire sauce

salt and freshly ground black pepper

Roast apples

4 ripe English Cox's apples

a little caster sugar

4 tbsp olive oil

1 Heat 100g (3½oz) unsalted butter in a large frying pan, add the onion and garlic and cook for 20 minutes, or until very soft, then cool

2 Meanwhile, mix the room-temperaure Stilton to a paste with the mustard, chilli, fennel and parsley. You could mix this using a food processor, but it makes it too smooth. Gradually mix in the cider brandy, Worcestershire sauce and some black pepper. Finally add the buttery, cooked onions and garlic and mix well. Check the seasoning.

3 Spoon into four small china pots or one large dish, then chill well.

4 Make some clarified butter by very gently warming the remaining butter in a small pan. The whey (the milky bit) will separate from the golden fat, dropping to the bottom of the pan. Spoon the fat only over the chilled pots or pot, and chill again.

5 Preheat the oven to 220°C/425°F/Gas 7.

6 Cut each of the apples in half and remove the core with a teaspoon or melon baller. Place on a non-stick baking tray. Sprinkle with a little salt, sugar and pepper then a drizzle of olive oil. Bake for 15 minutes, or until they start to puff nicely, almost soufflé. Do not overcook, they must still have a little bite. Cool.

7 Remove the potted Stilton from the fridge 30 minutes before you want to eat. The butter and cheese will soften perfectly. Serve with toast and two halves of roasted apple in the skin. Spoon a little potted cheese on to your toast, then top with a little roasted apple.

PORK PIES
DICKINSON & MORRIS

Research has shown that pork pies are often bought by blokes sent shopping by their wives and eaten as a guilty pleasure in the car on the way home. This furtiveness is a great pity because at its best the pork pie is a thing of glory, and a uniquely British invention.

The knowledge of who first sealed minced pork in a pastry case to cook is long lost. The first printed recipe dates back to the courtly cookbooks of Richard II's reign in 1390, when the pork pie was much more like the traditional spicy mince pie. Certainly the pork pie's unique affinity with Leicestershire, and in particular the charming market town of Melton Mowbray, dates back 200 years to when the pork pie became a popular snack for Midlands huntsmen. Today, a mere five companies still make pork pies (about 3 million of them a year) in the town.

Dickinson & Morris claims to be the oldest producer, having been on the same spot since 1851. They make 4,000 wonderfully traditional pork pies every week. I hooked up with managing director, Steve Hallam, who explained to me the three cardinal rules of the perfect pork pie: they have to be made from fresh, uncured pork; when they go in the oven, they receive no support from baking tins or hoops; and they have to come from Melton Mowbray, of course.

Master baker, Tony Wensley, then showed me how the Dickinson & Morris pork pie features equal amounts of pastry and filling. He measured out a pound 'billet' of lovely suety pastry, split it into two proper handfuls, and flattened these into fat discs. Then, using a traditional wooden dolly, which is similar to a stonemason's circular mallet, he made a deep indentation into the pastry disc. Pressing down on the dolly makes the soft pastry rise up round the sides. Under instruction, I helped smooth the pastry up the sides like a potter working clay, then removed the dolly to leave a thick pastry cup. The half-pound meatball is literally thrown into the pastry cup, then lidded over and crimped tight shut. Next, it's into the oven, unsupported, and as it bakes, the soft pastry sags, which gives the pie its characteristic barrel-shaped sides.

The sagging is partly caused by the expansion of the heated meat pushing the pie walls out. As it cools, the meat (but not the pastry) contracts, leaving a space. Back in the 18th century, pie-makers discovered that a jelly (made from long-boiled-up animal hooves) poured into the space between pastry and filling would preserve the finished pie for up to two months and lock in the filling's natural succulence and flavours. Today, little has changed at Dickinson & Morris, apart from the hygiene levels, I suspect. In the background of the kitchens every day is a saucepan of pigs' trotters boiling merrily. Steve showed me how they make two holes in the pork-pie lid: one to pour in the scalding liquid with a steady hand, the other to let the air out.

There's not much more to it apart from having the patience to let the pies cool. Years ago the pies would have been put straight into the fire and the scorched rock-hard pastry smashed and discarded to get at the meat. Today, the lard pastry is part of the whole glorious pork-pie experience and we scoff the lot, preferably with a jar of good English 'blow-your-socks-off' mustard to hand.

Pork pies are my dad's favourite snack and I must admit, after my visit to Melton Mowbray to eat the real thing fresh from the oven, I can see why.

July - We made pastry and pies by hand and boiled up pigs trotters for the jelly

COLD PORK PIE
WITH PICCALILLI

Serves: about 6-10

1 x 900g (2lb) large Melton Mowbray pork pie

Vegetables

250g (9oz) small pickling onions, peeled, or shallots, peeled and roughly chopped

300g (10½oz) small cauliflower florets

250g (9oz) cucumber, cut into 5mm (¼in) dice

250g (9oz) green beans, cut into 1cm (½in) pieces

1 tsp very finely chopped red chilli

Sauce

125g (4½oz) caster sugar

30g (1¼oz) plain flour

1½ tsp ground mace

1 tsp ground allspice

1 tbsp each of ground ginger and hot curry powder

2 tsp ground turmeric

3 heaped tbsp mustard powder

2 heaped tsp salt

600ml (1 pint) distilled malt vinegar

10g (¼oz) black peppercorns, crushed

2 tsp black mustard seeds

My father used to make piccalilli when were kids. I can still remember the whole house smelling of boiled vinegar and mustard. He would store it in old-fashioned glass jars from a lady called Mrs Pilcher, who owned a sweet shop. He would stack them in the garage, along with jars of pickled onions and red cabbage. He would eat this piccalilli with home-made brawn, something you hardly see these days. I like it with a cold Dickinson & Morris pork pie. The longer you can leave this pickle the better, for up to six months, but you must drain the vegetables well or the pickle will dilute and lose its preserving quality. I use ordinary brown vinegar, which is just perfect for the job.

1 Blanch all the vegetables in boiling water for 4 minutes, then drain and refresh under cold water. Do not overcook; they must have a crunch still. Drain very well on kitchen paper or clean tea-towel.

2 To make the sauce, place the sugar, flour, all the ground spices and salt into a bowl, and add enough vinegar to form a thickish paste.

3 Place the paste, the remaining vinegar, the peppercorns and mustard seeds into a saucepan and bring to the boil, then simmer for 3 minutes. Remove the pan from the heat, and leave to cool.

4 Add the drained vegetables to the sauce, and mix well. Cover and leave overnight.

5 The next day, mix well, and store in sterilized jars. The piccalilli can be eaten straightaway, but it's best to leave it for at least a couple of hours, or, better, a few days. The longer the better for the flavours to mature.

6 Serve with wedges of cold pork pie – delicious!

WARM PORK PIE WITH MUSHY PEAS

Serves: 4-6

1 x 900g (2lb) large Melton Mowbray pork pie

250g (9oz) green split peas or marrowfat peas

2 bicarbonate of soda tablets

55g (2oz) unsalted butter

2-3 pinches salt

freshly ground black pepper

Pork pie with mushy peas is unbeatable. But I get really fed up with going into restaurants or pubs these days and ordering so-called mushy peas, only to discover that they are frozen petits pois, boiled and mashed with mint, not mushy peas at all. Can we please start cooking real mushy peas? Blackpool chippies (and Lancashire chippies in general, actually) do real mushy peas, Swansea market do wonderful faggots with real mushy peas, and all these so-called chefs need to eat the real thing. There is much debate about mushy peas: green split, or marrowfat; soak them, don't soak them; soak them with bicarb, without bicarb; add salt when cooking, don't add salt; add mint sauce, butter etc. With so many variations I had to conduct a few tests. Firstly, I bought marrowfat peas, the ones that come with tablets of bicarbonate of soda. I soaked one with the bicarb and one without, for 12 hours. Then I rinsed them well, covered them with cold water, brought them to the boil and simmered for about 1 hour. The peas with bicarb broke down nicely, had a good colour and looked like real mushy peas. The ones without bicarb I cooked for a second hour: they were still like bullets and an awful colour.

I live now in a hard-water area, so I wonder if this has anything to do with it. Whilst I was in the West Country (soft-water area), our mushy peas were fine, and a great colour, with salt and without bicarb, but then I used green split peas, not marrowfat peas! The other point to mention is adding salt at the start. This can toughen the skins and, along with most other pulses such as butter beans, prolong the cooking time considerably. It can also make the pulses hard and inedible.

So, after all that, the choice really is yours. I have to say, I still like the bicarbed version, which taste great, and provided it's all part of a balanced diet, I don't have a problem with them. But for extra vitamins, which are nuked by bicarb, you're probably best off with green split peas. Below I give you recipes for both.

1 Soak both peas overnight in plenty of cold water. For the marrowfat, add the 2 bicarb tablets.

2 The next day, rinse the peas well in plenty of cold water. Place into a saucepan and cover with more cold water. Bring to the boil, then turn down the heat and simmer for about an hour. The peas will break up slightly, and you may have to add a touch of water to keep them soft.

3 Once cooked and nice and mushy, remove from the heat and add the butter, salt and pepper, and mix well. You may want to add a little more water. Cover and keep warm.

4 Serve with large chunks of pork pie, warmed slightly in a moderate oven, and red cabbage.

A lot has been written about chips over the past few years, some good, some bad, and some downright rubbish. Chips for me, fall into four categories: the chip shop; the frozen/microwavable ones that the fast food companies pump out; the frozen bake-straight-from-the-freezer ones; and good old-fashioned home-made. All four are completely different in every way, shape, form and cooking method. Whilst I can just about eat all four (I like the microwave ones least), I like the home-made variety the best. Having said that, chip-shop chips, smothered in gravy and mushy peas, are a delight when you are very hungry. The thin, crisp, French allumette-style ones the fast-food guys serve are very tasty; the trouble is they go cold too quickly.

I have spent many hours cooking and tasting chips over the years, using different oils, cooking times, potato varieties, temperatures etc., but I always come back to the basic recipe I was taught 25 years ago. That is, Maris Piper, King Edward or Désirée potatoes, good beef dripping, and cooked twice. The result is a well-coloured chip, which is nice and crisp on the outside and has a floury centre. It will keep warm for 20 minutes. The other secret is to never completely change the dripping. Once you have used the oil a few times, only remove three-quarters of it, then refill with fresh dripping. This ensures good flavour, crispness and colour. Chips are the perfect accompaniment to a great pork pie; the only other thing you need is a large blob of English mustard.

DRIPPING CHIPS

Serves: 4

4-5 large potatoes, peeled
2kg (4½lb) beef dripping
salt

1 Cut the potatoes into 1-1.5cm (½-⅝in) thick slices then into 10cm (4in) lengths (I like long chips). Wash well to remove the starch, then drain and dry with kitchen paper.

2 Heat the dripping to 145°C/293°F.

3 Add a quarter of the chips and cook for about 6-8 minutes, or until nice and cooked through, but with no colour and not falling apart. Remove the chips from the dripping to kitchen paper, and allow the dripping to reheat to the original temperature. Repeat the process for the remaining three batches.

4 Turn the heat up to 185-190°C/365-374°F.

5 This time fry the chips in two batches, for a couple of minutes only, to brown nicely.

6 Never cover, just sprinkle with salt and serve.

GAME

Game has been a big part of my life for many years. The first time I remember shooting game was poaching a hen partridge, with an air rifle, some 30 years ago, whilst I worked part-time on a farm.

By this time I knew I wanted to be a chef, and the only thing on my mind was to finish work, get home and cook my lovely bird. So I quickly cycled home with it tucked into my blue boiler-suit. Once home, I set about gleaning as much information from the only cookbook I had, Warne's *Everyday Cookery*, published in 1937 (I still have it to this day). In this, given to me by a caretaker from the church hall, are nearly 400 pages of recipes and fantastic colour plates. To a budding chef, this was compelling reading. There is a whole page on how to choose game and poultry, including hares and rabbits, moorhens, plovers, wheatears, ortolans and partridges. I studied the book carefully and decided I had a young English partridge!

I prepared and cooked the bird exactly how the book described, roasted with flat mushrooms, and served on a croûte of fried bread. As I ate my first game bird (it wasn't particularly good I recall, a bit dry and stringy), I felt at one with nature, almost the hunter-gatherer. Sounds a bit twee, but it's true, and my love of game had well and truly started.

Over the years I have been on many shoots, and the most important thing to me is to ensure that nothing gets wasted. At the end of any shoot, I used to gather up all the game the keeper had not sold or given to the guns, and take them back to the hotel or restaurant I was working at, and nothing was wasted: I would make terrines, pâtés, sausages, roasts, soups and stocks from all the bones. The law has changed slightly now, and you can't take any game to a restaurant or hotel kitchen: it all has to be prepared separately, and you have to have a game licence. Sadly, because of this, young chefs no longer see how to pluck and draw a bird, or understand the importance of hanging

Commercial shoots, which rear and release tens of thousands of birds, have become a large part of the rural economy, and many syndicates will pay handsomely to shoot driven pheasant and partridge. I have no problem with small shoots shooting small bags, provided all the game shot is collected, dispatched humanely and sold quickly. I do have an issue with huge shoots that will regularly shoot 1,000 birds a day. To me this is not real shooting, but mass destruction, with no real care for the quarry or the countryside.

Real shooting to me is what is called 'walking up' or 'rough shooting'. This is basically a couple of guns and a couple of dogs walking over rough ground. The occasional pheasant, partridge or, if you're lucky, a woodcock may be flushed out. I have been on shoots where the total bag for the day (eight hours' walking) has only been four pheasants and a woodcock. The bag is shared out at the end, and all go home tired but satisfied.

I have learned a lot about shooting and rearing of game from Bruce Laughton's keepers, Phil and Bomber, in Nottinghamshire. Theirs is a small, well-run, carefully managed shoot. It's so good to see real professionals caring not only about what they do, but also about how that business affects the countryside.

Game cookery to me is a fundamental part of the culinary year, and I will always cook and push game. It really has yet to take off in the UK. We touch on it, but don't embrace the variety and wonderful taste of our unique game. This chapter hopefully will get you cooking game dishes that are really tasty and different.

ROAST WILD DUCK CROWN WITH BEETROOT

Wild duck is one of my favourite game birds. Apart from grouse, wild duck and partridge herald the opening of the game season. 'Wild duck' is a general term for a huge array of species. There are hundreds, ranging from mallard, the ones at the local duck-pond with the blue-mauve feathers, to teal, very small, fast ducks, which fly straight up in the air when disturbed. They are delicious when cooked correctly, but they have very little natural fat and will dry out if not respected. Ask your butcher to remove the crown – the breasts on the bone, with wishbone removed (easier to carve) – and to chop the carcass, legs, and rib-cage, into small pieces. This simple recipe is perfect with a beautiful, deep-coloured sauce.

Serves: 2

2 wild mallard crowns

the rest of the duck carcasses, including the legs, cut into small pieces

1 carrot, peeled and roughly chopped

½ onion, peeled and finely chopped

2 small raw beetroots, peeled and cut into 8 wedges

600ml (1 pint) strong chicken stock

2 tbsp red wine vinegar

175ml (6fl oz) dry white wine

2 tbsp vegetable oil

salt and freshly ground black pepper

15g (½oz) unsalted butter

1 Preheat the oven to 230°C/450°F/Gas 8.

2 Place the carcass bones and legs, carrot and onion into a roasting tray. Cook in the oven for about 30 minutes, or until well browned.

3 Put the beetroots into the chicken stock and simmer for 20 minutes, or until cooked, but not overcooked. Some beetroots take longer than others, so keep checking. Once cooked, remove the beetroots from the stock and reserve, covered. Chop into cubes if you like.

4 Meanwhile, carefully remove the wish-bone from the neck of the crown, by running a sharp knife down each side of the bone and pulling the bone out gently.

5 Once the bones and vegetables have browned, pop into a small saucepan. Add the vinegar and wine and cook down until the liquid has almost evaporated.

6 Add the beetroot-chicken stock, and cook for 20 minutes to get the flavour out of the bones, skimming off any fat or debris occasionally.

7 Strain the stock into a clean pan, and simmer down, again skimming occasionally to remove any fat, until you have a nice, deep-flavoured, syrupy sauce. If the fat boils into the sauce it can turn cloudy.

8 Heat the vegetable oil in a ovenproof frying pan. Season the duck well, inside and out, with salt and pepper. Place skin-side down into the hot oil, cook for 1 minute, then place straight into the hot oven. Cook for 6-8 minutes, then turn the crown over and cook for a further 6 minutes.

9 Once cooked, remove the pan from the oven (the duck will still be

slightly undercooked at this stage), turn the crowns back on to the skin, cover with foil, and leave to rest for 15 minutes, while you finish the sauce.

10 Add the cooked beetroot to the stock, with the butter and stir in. The butter will thicken the sauce slightly, and also give the sauce a brilliant sheen.

11 Check the duck is cooked by piercing it in a thick place to ensure the juices run clear. Carve the breasts off the bone, which will be perfectly cooked, pink and delicious, and slice each side into two to three slices. Place on a plate and spoon over the beetroot sauce. Serve with creamy mashed potatoes, and some braised Savoy cabbage.

PHEASANT CURRY

Serves: 2

2 young pheasants, cocks or hens, skinned

3 tbsp vegetable oil

1 tbsp black mustard seeds

1 tbsp black onion seeds

6 garlic cloves, peeled and chopped

1 tbsp chopped fresh red chilli

1 tsp ground cumin

1 tsp ground turmeric

a pinch of saffron strands

10 curry leaves

1 tbsp peeled and finely chopped fresh root ginger

2 small onions, peeled and finely chopped

125g (4½oz) dry-cure streaky bacon, cut into 2cm (¾in) pieces

1 chicken stock cube

300ml (10fl oz) lager

salt and freshly ground black pepper

a pinch of caster sugar

250g (9oz) fresh ripe tomatoes, chopped

70g (2½oz) sultanas

To serve

3 tbsp chopped coriander

2 tbsp chopped mint

4 tbsp double cream

Pheasant is one of the most under-used meats around: the birds are cheap, lean and very tasty. I have spent a long time trying all different ways of cooking pheasant perfectly and, along with guinea fowl, I have found it very difficult to get right consistently for quite a few reasons. Firstly, how old is the bird? It could be this year's young thing, or last year's, or even five years old, and is it a cock or a hen? One way of adding different flavours to pheasant is to curry it. The strong flavour of well-hung pheasant really lends itself well to curry flavours. Couple that with a little sweetness from the sultanas, and a good soaking in lager and, hey presto, a superb dish. This could be a great pub dish of the future.

1 Remove the legs and breasts from the pheasants. Chop off the feet and discard the drumstick. Remove the sinew from the inner fillet of the breasts, also from the larger part of the breast meat. Bone out the thighs and reserve the meat. Cut up both sets of meat into 4cm (1½in) chunks, but keep them separate: this is because we need to cook the thighs for a longer period of time, especially on an older cock bird, as the meat tends to be tougher. Cover the breast meat and refrigerate.

2 Heat the oil in a saucepan, add the mustard and onion seeds, garlic, chilli, all the ground spices, saffron, curry leaves and fresh ginger. Cook over a low heat to release the flavours, but do not overheat or the spices will burn. Add the onion and bacon and cook to soften slightly.

3 Add the pheasant thigh meat, and stir to coat in the onion and spices.

4 Add the stock cube, lager, salt and pepper, sugar, tomatoes and sultanas.

5 Bring to the boil, then turn the heat down to a simmer and half-cover with a lid. Cook for 1¼ hours.

6 Stir occasionally, then at the 1¼ hour mark, drop in the pheasant breast and stir through.

7 Cook for a further 15 minutes, or until the breast is just cooked. Do not overcook the breast or it will dry out. By now the sauce should be thick and full of flavour and colour. Remove the pot from the stove, and stir in the coriander, mint and double cream.

8 Serve with plain boiled rice, natural yoghurt and chapatti.

PHEASANT, BLACK PUDDING AND BRAMLEY APPLE PARCELS

Serves: 4

8 tbsp good-quality jarred or canned sauerkraut

3 pinches caster sugar

salt and freshly ground black pepper

8 pheasant thighs, skinned and boned

8 filo sheets, cut to 23 x 18cm (9 x 7in) approx.

unsalted butter, melted

8 thick slices good-quality black pudding

1 large Bramley apple, peeled, cored whole, and cut into 8 rings

The trendy way of cooking pheasants these days is to only use the breasts. Not too sure about this, but I can see the reason why. It's notoriously difficult to roast a whole pheasant consistently well. Because most birds are wet-plucked, then stuffed into plastic trays and tightly wrapped in clingfilm, you really have no idea what you are buying.

Hanging is another bone of contention. You hear great old tales like 'hang it by the head until it falls to the ground' or 'hang them until they're green and full of maggots.' Yeah, right. A couple of days in October is fine, and perhaps a day or two extra when the weather cools down. That will give you an all-round, nicely gamey flavour.

Mostly the legs are used to make stock or sauce. Here, you can use the breasts for one dish, and legs cooked this way get a second meal out of the bird. The use of filo pastry is often seen as a bit naff, and has been greatly over-used, I know. I use the buttered filo to hold in the steam so the legs gently cook, and the butter keeps the pastry crisp. It's a novel way of using up the thighs, and they are moist and tender.

1 Preheat the oven to 200°C/400°F/Gas 6.

2 Spoon the sauerkraut into a saucepan, add the sugar and cook until all the moisture has been driven off. Add a good seasoning of salt and pepper, and leave to cool.

3 Using a sharp knife, make a few incisions across the flesh of one of the thighs and repeat with all the thighs.

4 Lay out two slices of the filo pastry and brush with melted butter. Lay the filo sheets on top of each other. Lay a thigh on top in the middle and season well with salt and pepper. Top with two small spoons of sauerkraut, two slices of black pudding and two apple rings. Top with the other thigh and season well, then fold up into a nice tight parcel. Do the same with the remaining ingredients to make four filo parcels.

5 Brush with melted butter and season well with salt and black pepper. Bake for 35-40 minutes, until cooked. Serve straight away with spiced Victoria plum sauce.

STEAMED HARE AND
MEDLAR JELLY PUDDING

Fills: 1 x 22 x 10cm (8½ x 4in) deep
Pyrex bowl, to serve 8

Filling

1 large hare, skinned and gutted, to
give you 750g (1lb 10oz) hare meat, cut
into 2cm (¾in) cubes

2 tbsp plain flour

salt and freshly ground black pepper

6 tbsp vegetable oil

100g (3½oz) streaky bacon, cut into
2cm (¾in) pieces

2 large onions, peeled and chopped

2 garlic cloves, peeled and chopped

2 celery stalks, chopped

approx. 600ml (1 pint) strong game
or beef stock

150ml (5fl oz) red wine

2 tbsp gin

3 tbsp medlar jelly

1 tbsp Worcestershire sauce

6 juniper berries

2 bay leaves

3 x 6cm sprigs fresh rosemary

Parsley suet pastry

225g (8oz) self-raising flour

2 pinches salt

6 heaped tbsp chopped parsley

115g (4oz) beef suet

1 medium egg, lightly beaten

approx. 2 tbsp cold water

unsalted butter, for greasing

*Not often seen these days, but a real gem in the game calendar. I first cooked this
pudding in 1979, and it blew me away. I had only ever eaten jugged hare, and not
a very well prepared one at that. The long slow cooking process really helps to bring
out the flavour of the hare. It's quite a distinct flavour, and can be very strong. But
if you balance that with the sweetness of the medlar jelly and the pungency of the
gin and rosemary, it's spectacular. Remember to make the pastry just before you
cook. This is a take on suet pastry, to which I add an egg for a tighter end-result,
especially when it has to hold in quite a lot of filling. Overwork the pastry slightly
to break down the suet.*

1 Place a steamer pan on the stove and half fill with cold water. Bring to
the boil, then simmer with a lid on.

2 Toss the diced hare in the flour, and season with a little salt and
pepper. Meanwhile, heat 4 tbsp of the vegetable oil in a large frying pan.
Add the meat to the oil and brown for 3-4 minutes over a high heat.
Remove from the hot oil and reserve in a bowl or dish.

3 Add the remaining oil and the streaky bacon to the pan, and cook for
10 minutes to let the bacon take some colour and release its fat. Again,
remove the bacon and add to the sealed hare.

4 Add the onion, garlic and celery to the pan, and cook for 10 minutes
to soften and take on a little colour.

5 Meanwhile, make the pastry. Place the flour, salt, parsley, suet and egg
in a mixing bowl and mix well. Add a touch of cold water and mix to a
soft, but not sticky dough. Roll out nice and thin, about 3mm (⅛in), and
use straightaway as the raising agents are working away.

6 Line a well-buttered 1.3kg (3lb) Pyrex bowl with two-thirds of the
pastry. Leave plenty hanging over the top edge. Place the sealed hare,
celery, onion, garlic and bacon into the lined bowl.

7 Bring the stock, red wine, gin, jelly, Worcestershire sauce and juniper
berries to the boil in a medium pan, then fill up the pudding, right to the
top. Leave about 2cm (¾in) free. Top with the rosemary and bay leaves.

8 Roll out the last piece of pastry. Wet the top rim of the bowl, and
crimp the top on securely. Make a small incision to let out the steam.

9 Carefully wrap in a double layer of well-buttered foil and secure well. Check the simmering water in the steamer base is still at least half full.

10 Place the pudding in the steamer tray and cover tightly. Simmer for at least 4 hours, checking the water level every 30-40 minutes. Top up with boiling water from a boiling kettle. This keeps the water simmering all the time.

11 After 4 hours, remove the pudding from the steamer, and leave to cool for 30 minutes. Remove the foil, and turn out on to a hot serving plate or dish. Spoon over the thick game gravy, cut into eight wedges, and serve with mashed potatoes and mustard kale.

POACHED AND MARINATED WILD RABBIT

Serves: 6

2 small wild rabbits, or 1 large domestic rabbit, skinned and gutted

4 bay leaves

2 chicken stock cubes

2 large sprigs fresh rosemary

1 tbsp salt

4 tbsp finely chopped fresh sage

4 pinches cracked black pepper

480ml (17fl oz) extra virgin olive oil, warmed

I went often to a restaurant in Asti, northern Italy, and had this dish every time. It's one of the nicest rabbit dishes I have ever tasted. It's so simple, it's almost unbelievable. The secrets are, firstly, to just simmer the rabbit, or the meat will toughen and dry out. You must also make sure the oil is the same temperature as the meat, and leave for 48 hours in the fridge. Finally, when you want to eat, remove the rabbit from the fridge and allow it to come to room temperature, then season with salt and pepper. You can also warm it slightly in a pan, but do not overheat.

1 Cut the rabbits into three: back legs, back, and front legs. Place in a large saucepan, cover with cold water and add the bay leaves, stock cubes, rosemary and ½ tbsp salt. Bring to the boil and then just simmer for 1 hour with a lid on. This is really important: the pan must just simmer or the saddles will dry out very quickly. Check the meat is cooked through.

2 Strain off the stock and discard. Carefully remove all the hot meat from the carcass. Try to leave the meat in good-sized pieces; this makes the end result more appealing.

3 Place the meat into a deep bowl and add the chopped sage, black pepper and the remaining salt and mix well. Finally pour over the warm oil, and carefully mix so as not to break up the warm meat. Cover with clingfilm (it's important to cover the meat completely), then leave to cool. Pop into the fridge and leave for a couple of days to marinate.

4 Serve slightly warmed with watercress, char-grilled, crisp bread, roughly chopped chives and some warm roasted English bunch carrots.

ENGLISH MUSTARD CURLY KALE FOR GAME

Kale is not often seen these days, and is mostly used for cattle fodder, which is a shame because this superb winter vegetable is a wonderful accompaniment to braises, casseroles, stews and puddings. The secret (which goes against all the cooking vegetable rules) is to slightly overcook it. Some of you may disagree, but I think the taste and texture is so much better once it is slightly overcooked, although not soggy. This vegetable dish also works well with most game dishes, including pheasant curry and wild duck with beetroots.

Serves: 4

2 x 150g (5½oz) bags curly kale
salt and freshly ground black pepper
55g (2oz) unsalted butter or 4 tbsp extra virgin olive oil
4 tbsp English mustard powder, reconstituted, not too thin

1 Pick over the kale and rip out any tough stalks. Wash really well in a couple of changes of cold water. Meanwhile, bring a large pan of water to the boil and season with salt.

2 Pile the kale into the rapidly boiling water and stir well. Be careful here as the kale will overcook quite quickly. Cook for about 3-4 minutes only, or until soft but still green.

3 Drain the kale and refresh under cold running water. Squeeze out the kale (not too tightly) and leave in four to six small balls.

4 When you come to warm the kale, place the butter or olive oil in a wok and heat through. Add the kale and season well, then stir gently to warm through – don't let the kale catch. Finally, stir in the English mustard (it's up to you how much you use) and serve straightaway.

SPICED PLUM SAUCE FOR GAME

We always seem to have a glut of plums, and this is a nice way to preserve some for the onset of winter. This will be great with all game dishes, including terrines, pâtés and even sausages and pork pies. If you missed the plum season, then plums from abroad are OK, but at a pinch. Failing that, semi-dried or dried varieties work well.

Serves: 4-6

4 tbsp vegetable oil
1 small onion, peeled and finely chopped
2 garlic cloves, peeled
1 tbsp finely chopped fresh root ginger
2 tbsp ground cinnamon
55g (2oz) light brown demerara sugar
350g (12oz) Victoria plums, stoned
3 tbsp sherry vinegar
300ml (10fl oz) strong chicken or vegetable stock
2 pinches sea salt
2 pinches ground black pepper

1 Heat the vegetable oil in a saucepan, then add the onion, garlic, ginger, cinnamon and sugar, and cook over a low heat for 2-3 minutes.

2 Add the plums, vinegar, stock, salt and pepper, and cook for 20 minutes, or until the plums are soft and pulpy. The longer you cook the sauce, the thicker it will be.

3 Liquidize and pass through a fine sieve. Season again if needed, and serve warm, or cooled and chilled.

ROAST PARTRIDGE WITH GRAPES AND ALMONDS

This recipe is slightly cheffy – by which I mean it involves careful cooking, with a sauce made to order, and the meat is fairly pink. Don't worry, it's still very simple, and the delicate flavour and juiciness of the partridge is delicious. The secret to cooking any game bird is to slightly undercook, then rest it.

Serves: 1

30g (1¼oz) unsalted butter

1 tbsp vegetable oil

1 English partridge, wish-bone removed

salt and freshly ground black pepper

2 tsp white wine vinegar

125ml (4fl oz) medium white wine

1 shallot, peeled and finely chopped

300ml (10fl oz) fairly strong chicken stock

a pinch of caster sugar

6-8 white seedless grapes, sliced in half

2 tbsp flaked almonds, lightly browned

1 Preheat the oven to 220°C/425°F/Gas 7. Heat 25g (1oz) of the butter and the oil in an ovenproof frying or sauté pan. Once foaming, lightly season the bird all over with a little salt and pepper. Place leg-side down in the pan, brown for a minute or so, then roast for 5 minutes.

2 Remove the bird from the oven and turn on to the other leg. Spoon over the buttery juices and oil, return to the oven, and roast for a further 5 minutes. Remove the pan from the oven, place the bird breast-side down and return to the oven for 3 minutes, again spooning over the buttery juices.

3 Once the bird is cooked through, remove the pan from the oven, take the partridge out of the pan, place on a warm plate, and cover with foil. Leave to rest in a warm place for 6-8 minutes. After this time, place the bird on a chopping board, breast-side up.

4 Run a sharp knife through where the leg is attached to the breast, then carefully pull the leg away from the body of the bird. Repeat this for the other leg. Keep the legs warm. The meat will be pink and juicy. Run the knife down the breast-bone, as close as possible, right down to where the wing is attached. Cut through the joint where the wing is attached to the breast, and carefully pull off the breast meat. Repeat on the other side. Place on to the legs and keep warm, covered with foil.

5 Make the sauce by placing the carcass into a small saucepan, then adding the vinegar, white wine and shallot. Bring to the boil and boil until almost all the wine has evaporated. Add the chicken stock and sugar and bring to the boil. Simmer until thick and syrupy, about 5-6 minutes. Finally add the remaining butter and mix well, then strain through a fine sieve. Place in a clean saucepan and add the grapes, almonds and a touch of salt and pepper to taste.

6 Place the warm partridge legs on the plate, crossed at the top. Place the breasts on top of the legs, and carefully spoon over the hot sauce. Serve with small roasted potatoes and mustard kale.

WALES

LAMB
BRAISED SHOULDER OF LAMB WITH TOMATO AND HERBS

Serves: 4-6

1 small shoulder of Welsh lamb, or hogget, both tunnel-boned

4 celery stalks

2 small carrots

1 large onion, peeled and finely chopped

1 medium leek, split and washed well

500ml (18fl oz) dry white wine

4 heaped tsp caster sugar

salt and freshly ground black pepper

1 sprig rosemary

2 bay leaves

leaves from 1 sprig thyme

4 garlic cloves, peeled and crushed

approx. 2 litres (3½ pints) each of well-flavoured lamb and brown chicken stock

a little arrowroot or cornflour, slaked in water

To finish

2 ripe plum tomatoes, chopped

2 tbsp each of chopped basil, parsley and tarragon

2 heaped tbsp chopped thyme leaves

This recipe needs to be made a day in advance, so the meat can chill well. It does take a bit of time to prepare but is well worth it. The cooked joint will keep in the chilled stock for up to a week in the fridge.

1 Preheat the oven to 170°C/325°F/Gas 3.

2 Wash and chop all the vegetables into 2cm (¾in) pieces.

3 Bring the white wine to the boil in a large, deep ovenproof pan and add the sugar and a little salt and pepper. Add the vegetables, rosemary and bay leaves, and stir well. Keep at a simmer.

4 Next, season the shoulder of lamb well inside and out with salt and pepper. Mix the thyme and garlic together and smear a generous amount inside the cavity of the shoulder. Then roll the shoulder up, making sure the open end of the shoulder is to your left, or right. Tie securely, by starting at the centre, then moving to both ends to seal. Then fill in the gaps evenly. There should be a tie every 1cm (½in).

5 Place the lamb into the vegetables and liquid in the pan, and pour on enough stock, in equal amounts, to just cover the shoulder. Season well and taste. You may need to add a touch more sugar: the stock must be not only well flavoured, but also well balanced, by which I mean sweet enough, meaty enough, seasoned properly and the right colour. Keep tasting.

6 Bring the stock and lamb to the boil on the stove, cover and place in the preheated oven. Cook until a skewer can be inserted right through the joint with only a little resistance, which will take about 3 hours, provided the stock was simmering when the pan was placed in the oven. When cooked there will be a wonderful aroma around the kitchen.

7 Remove the pan from the oven and cool. Then chill the whole pan in the fridge so the meat cools down totally immersed in the stock. This is very important as it helps to keep as much flavour in the joint as possible.

8 When chilled, the joint will set completely. Remove from the stock and rinse under cold water to get rid of any set fat. Carefully remove the strings, wrap in clingfilm and place back into the fridge.

9 Remove all traces of solidified fat from the top of the stock and throw away, as you don't want any trace of grease in the sauce. Warm the stock and strain through a fine sieve so you are left with a beautifully coloured and flavoured stock. Taste and see what you think. If you are happy with the flavour, then boil and thicken slightly with a little slaked arrowroot or cornflour. I personally like a rich dark sauce for this type of dish so I carefully bring the stock back to the boil and reduce slowly until it reaches the required colour and texture.

10 Strain again and add most of the chopped tomatoes, basil, parsley, tarragon and thyme. Cover and leave to infuse for 30-40 minutes.

11 Meanwhile, cut the lamb into 4cm (1½in) thick slices and arrange in a tray. Strain the stock and re-season if needed. Spoon enough hot sauce over the lamb to coat, cover with foil and pop into the oven preheated to 200°C/400°F/Gas 6 for about 25 minutes.

12 Serve the lamb with boiled, minted, buttered new potatoes, plenty of buttered spinach and plenty of sauce, garnished with the remaining tomato and herbs.

COTTAGE PIE WITH SPICY HERB TOPPING

Serves: 4

500g (18oz) lean lamb mince

2 tbsp olive oil

1 small onion, peeled and chopped

1 tsp fresh thyme leaves

4 heaped tbsp plain flour

2 tbsp tomato ketchup

1 tbsp Worcestershire sauce

350ml (12fl oz) strong lamb or chicken stock

Aubergine

1 aubergine

6 tbsp olive oil

Spicy herb topping

about 1kg (2¼lb) potatoes, peeled

200ml (7fl oz) warm milk

100g (3¼oz) butter, melted

1 tsp curry powder

1 tsp paprika

4 tbsp roughly chopped parsley

salt and freshly ground black pepper

Perfect for the early autumn, this twist on cottage pie is a real winner in the Vickery household.

1 Preheat the oven to 220°C/425°F/Gas 7.

2 Heat the oil in a saucepan. Add the onion and thyme and cook for 5 minutes to colour slightly, then add the mince and also colour slightly. Add the flour and let the bottom catch slightly but do not burn; this adds to the flavour, I promise. Then add the ketchup and Worcestershire sauce and mix well.

3 Finally, pour in the stock, bring to a very low simmer and cook for 10–12 minutes.

4 Slice the aubergine into very thin rings and cook on both sides in the olive oil for a couple of minutes to colour slightly and soften. Then place on a piece of kitchen paper to drain well.

5 Meanwhile, boil the potatoes until very soft and well cooked, then strain.

6 Break up with a masher and keep warm. Place the warm mash into a bowl and add the warmed milk, butter, curry powder, paprika and chopped parsley, and season with salt and pepper.

7 Place half the mince into a baking dish about 30 x 20cm (12 x 8in). Lay over the cooked aubergines, add the rest of the mince and pipe or spread over the mash.

8 Bake for 30 minutes to brown and crisp well.

9 Once cooked, this dish will freeze very successfully. Cool well, wrap in clingfilm and freeze. To cook, remove from the freezer and defrost well, best overnight in the fridge. Then place in a preheated oven at 220°C/425°F/Gas 7 for 40 minutes or until very hot and glazed. Serve with a crisp green salad.

LAMB SOUP WITH MINT OIL

Serves: 6

500g (18oz) boned shoulder of Welsh lamb, cut into 4cm (1½in) chunks and most of the fat removed

4 tbsp sea salt

1 lamb or chicken stock cube

2 medium onions, peeled and chopped

2 bay leaves

2 carrots, peeled and chopped

1 head garlic, halved

20 black peppercorns

2 medium potatoes, peeled and cut into chunks.

salt and freshly ground black pepper

Mint oil

6 tbsp olive oil

10 leaves of mint

This is my version of a wonderful soup known as Reestit mutton that is traditionally served in the Shetland Islands. I had some recently and it was delicious. In the Shetlands they use salted and dried mutton to flavour the soup so if you can get one-year-old hogget or mutton this will give a much deeper flavour. This dish is tasty and nutritious; the addition of vegetables and potatoes makes it particularly hearty and filling.

1 Place the lamb into an earthenware dish, add the sea salt and mix well. Cover and leave for 24 hours in the fridge, turning occasionally.

2 The next day, place the meat into a sieve and rinse well, then pop into a saucepan, cover with cold water and bring to the boil. Skim well and add the stock cube then simmer for 30 minutes, skimming all the time.

3 Skim well then add the rest of the flavouring ingredients and simmer for a further 1½ hours, skimming all the time. The secret is to have no trace of fat on the end-product. By this time the meat will be very tender and starting to break up. Season well with pepper and salt if needed.

4 Remove the garlic head and bay leaves.

5 Add mint and olive oil. If you wish, place in a the liquidizer and blitz until smooth. Serve the soup in a bowl with a drizzle of mint oil.

CAERPHILLY CHEESE

GORWYDD CAERPHILLY

Gorwydd Farm lies on a remote Glamorganshire hillside. Its 100 acres of farmland is used for grazing but the real labour of love takes place in the outbuildings by the main farmhouse. Here the Trethowan family has been making wonderful Caerphilly cheese by hand for the past eight years.

Every day, seven days a week, brothers Todd and Maugan Trethowan and the latter's wife Kim take in 1500 litres of milk from a nearby farm and later, much later as we shall see, it leaves in the form of wonderful, mature truckles of cheese.

Todd learnt his trade in a very traditional way, apprenticed to such great cheese-makers as Chris Duckett down in Somerset. Caerphilly seemed the obvious cheese to make for geographical reasons, and because there weren't many people making it back then. Todd's first batch was a roaring success, being snapped up by the Neal's Yard cheese shop in London. Thereafter he was joined in the business by Maugan and Kim.

Unbelievably, every part of the cheese-making process is done by hand, and it's backbreaking work. The milk comes unpasteurized, which means that Trethowan's dairy has to be scrupulously clean. The yoghurt-like starter culture that kicks off the cheese-making process is relatively high in acidity and that helps control possible harmful bugs in the raw milk. Todd explained to me that the correct balance of acidity in the treated milk is vital. It's the foundation of the whole cheese, and they proceed no further until they have got this bit right.

Vegetarian rennet is added to the huge wooden vat and within an hour the concoction has the consistency of pallid blancmange. Maugan hunches over the vat, lovingly combing it with a stainless-steel rake to gently break up the curds and to release the waste liquid, the whey. At this stage, whoever's around has to scrub-up to the shoulders with the diligence of a surgeon and get stuck in – literally – to knead more moisture out of the warm curds with large paddles. I had a go and my back was soon protesting at having to lean over so far into the vat. Hand-working the cheese-to-be keeps in some of the succulence and open texture that industrial machine-milling would lose.

When ready, the sopping curds are poured into endless muslin-lined moulds. The Trethowans can make 40 x 4kg (9lb) cheeses from their daily delivery of milk. The cheeses are loaded into a hand-operated press to have more moisture squeezed out of them, and are then left for 14 hours. After that, the muslin is removed, they are brined for 24 hours, then they are rested for three months (a really long time for this kind of cheese).

Todd took me into one of the storage sheds. There were racks of beautiful Caerphilly rounds, which are turned every day to stop them sticking, to keep the moisture spreading through the cheese, and to stop the top drying out and cracking. The rapidly forming crusts are also rubbed by hand to remove excess mould which, although adding flavour, might endanger the cheese inside.

Finally, I was given a sliver of the beautifully pale, creamy, still crumbly cheese to try, and it was delicious – quite lemony and acidic, with a marked strength that surprises given the innocuous colour. You can safely eat the rind too and that gives a contrasting earthy, mushroomy flavour.

The supermarkets may be too profit-hungry to wait for their Caerphilly to mature but to my mind Trethowan's Caerphilly is well worth tracking down at the deli. I even found some as far away as Lincoln the other day, so it is out there.

CAERPHILLY AND WILD GARLIC TART

Serves: 6-8

1 x blind-baked shortcrust pastry flan or tart case, 24cm (9½in) in diameter and 4cm (1½in) deep (see page 17)

Filling

25g (1oz) unsalted butter

8 shallots, peeled and finely chopped

4 tbsp roughly chopped wild garlic leaves

2 tbsp roughly chopped parsley

4 tbsp roughly chopped chives

300g (10½oz) Caerphilly cheese, cut into small cubes

2 medium eggs, plus 2 medium egg yolks

600ml (1 pint) milk

½ tsp freshly grated nutmeg

salt and freshly ground black pepper

Sauce

2 shallots, peeled and roughly chopped

a few white peppercorns, crushed

a pinch of saffron stamens

4 tbsp white wine

4 tbsp white wine vinegar

2 medium egg yolks, at room temperature

85g (3oz) unsalted butter, melted

Ramsons, or wild garlic, is quite trendy now; various companies sell it over the internet and it's readily available. When I lived in the West Country, I would walk my dog along the banks of the river Tone and in March and April the whole bank would be covered with the stuff. I would pick the white flowers for salads and freeze the leaves for later use as the season is so short. The frozen leaves were quite good but not a patch on the fresh. Failing that, a mixture of a little garlic sautéed with the shallots, along with some baby spinach and basil leaves, is a successful substitute.

1 Preheat the oven to 200°C/400°F/Gas 6.

2 Heat the butter in a pan, add the shallot and gently cook for 15 minutes.

3 Spread the cooked shallots over the entire base of the pastry case. Sprinkle over the wild garlic and herbs, then top with the cheese. Pack the cheese in; you may want to add a touch more.

4 Beat the eggs and egg yolks with the milk, and season with nutmeg, salt and pepper. Pour some of this over the cheese, but only half fill. Place the flan on a baking tray then place in the oven. Now fill the flan to the top: this way, you don't get any spillage. Bake for 25-30 minutes, but do not overcook or the custard will puff up and soufflé.

5 Meanwhile make the sauce. Place the shallot, peppercorns, saffron, wine and vinegar into a pan. Bring to the boil and simmer rapidly to reduce by half. Strain and pour into a heatproof bowl. Add the egg yolks and whisk straightaway.

6 Place the bowl over a pan of gently simmering water (the bowl must not touch the water), and carry on whisking to cook the yolks until they are foamy, about 3-4 minutes. The foam will then start to thicken, at which point take off the heat, add a little of the butter and whisk well. Add the rest of the butter and whisk well again. You may need to add a touch of water to let the sauce down slightly if it is too thick.

7 Once the flan is cooked, remove from the oven. The middle should be slightly undercooked, which is fine. Leave to cool for 30 minutes, then pour the sauce over the top to cover it, and fill the pastry case. Place under a preheated grill until golden brown. Cut into slices to serve.

ARTICHOKE, LEMON AND CAERPHILLY SALAD

Some chefs will not use anything that comes from a jar, can or freezer, purely on principle; fair enough. But some products are pretty good and work quite well, like frozen peas and broad beans. Canned pulses are an OK substitute, if you can't wait two days to soak and cook the dried variety. Jarred artichokes, which are eaten all over Italy, are pretty good too. Here they are combined with creamy, pungent Caerphilly and lemon to make a good simple summer starter or main course.

Serves: 4

1 garlic clove, peeled and crushed

4 tbsp extra virgin olive oil

finely grated zest and juice of 1 large unwaxed lemon

2 tbsp chopped mint

2 tbsp roughly chopped parsley

3 x 285g (10oz) jars cooked artichokes, well drained

1 x 400g (16oz) can cannellini beans, well drained and rinsed

175g (6oz) Caerphilly cheese, cubed

salt and freshly ground black pepper

1 Mix the garlic with the olive oil, lemon zest and juice and chopped herbs.

2 Mix together the artichokes, beans and cheese, then add the oil mixture and combine well. Season well and leave for 1 hour at room temperature.

3 Serve piled bowls, with crusty bread.

CAERPHILLY AND SMOKED PAPRIKA DIP

This dip I picked up when I was in America about 10 years ago, so I cannot take the credit for it. The lady's name was Diane Dodge, and I went to a birthday party at her very nice woodland home. The highlight of the party was her onion dip. The original recipe used an American Cheddar, but I have adapted it to use Caerphilly, and it works a treat. This dip is sweet, melting and delicious, and perfect as nibbly starter with a glass of wine, beer or cider.

Serves: 6-8

55g (2oz) unsalted butter

3 medium onions, peeled and finely chopped

2 garlic cloves, peeled and crushed

225g (8oz) Caerphilly cheese, grated

225g (8oz) good-quality mayonnaise

1 tsp Tabasco sauce

1 tbsp Worcestershire sauce

1 tsp caster sugar

salt and freshly ground black pepper

3 tbsp sweet smoked paprika

1 Preheat the oven to 180°C/350°F/Gas 4.

2 Heat the butter in a pan, add the onion and garlic and cook gently for about 15 minutes to soften. Remove from the heat and stir in the Caerphilly, mayonnaise, sauces, sugar and finally a good seasoning of salt and pepper.

3 Place in a ceramic baking dish, sprinkle liberally and evenly with the paprika, and bake for 20 minutes.

4 Remove and allow to cool slightly. This should be eaten warm, not hot. Serve with crackers, slices of crunchy bread or breadsticks.

EAST
ANGLIA

CRABS
CROMER CRABS

The shores of south-west and north Norfolk are places of great bounty for fisherman, and prized above all are the plump, meat-packed brown crabs. Both coastlines claim theirs are the best in Britain. To find out, I headed up to north Norfolk to meet up with Gary Meers and Richard Matthews, who fish the treacherous North Sea off Sheringham.

When I innocently asked Gary if he fished in his open boat in the rain, he roared with laughter. There isn't much weather that Gary and Rich don't face head-on at sea. The forecast has to be pretty atrocious to drive Gary to his other job of reed cutting for thatch. The crabs used to disappear in September, effectively ending the fishermen's season, but today there are enough off the coast to merit fishing until December.

The day I visited Weybourne beach was beautiful and still, the sea mercifully calm. Gary and I flung the faded lifejackets and gear into his traditional wooden Cromer crabbing boat and clambered in over the steep clinker-built side while Richard drove the ancient tank-tracked tractor that nudged the sturdy open boat, none too delicately, over the shale down into the sea. Richard waded out to join us before we headed out a mile or so off the coast. It's thought crabs favour rocky sea-beds, making the gently shelving terrain off Norfolk ideal crab-hunting territory.

I was getting quite excited as the electric winch hauled in the first of a chain – a 'shank' – of 300 dripping pots Gary and Richard had laid two days before. Few came out of the

sea with no crabs inside, but one or two held lobsters as a bonus. The pair of fisherman haul the pots in over the side, wrest any catch from the cage, taking care to avoid finger-crushing pincers, re-bait the cage with horse mackerel, and release it over the side again.

Gary and Richard are scrupulous about the size of crab they catch, using a stainless-steel caliper to measure the shell to ensure it meets the minimum 12cm (4⅔in) across the back. Smaller crabs are flung back to face another day. Fast growers, they can be up to a full 20cm (8in) in another fortnight or so.

Up in Norfolk Gary and his cronies refer to male and female crabs as 'jacks' and 'broadsters'. In the West Country, where I used to buy crabs for my kitchen, the males are 'cocks' and the smaller females are called 'hens'. Regardless, they are the same species: brown or edible crabs, *Cancer pagurus*. They have a lovely ochre shell with pie-crust creasing around the edge, and are heavy with the promise of lovely meat.

Back on land the haul was unloaded and Richard's wife Alison cooked and dressed some on the spot. These are carted off for sale here in Norfolk. Many Cromer crabs end up in London or even abroad, where the brown crab is rightly prized over and above the spider crab, which doesn't give up its meat without a struggle. Not like these British beauties!

Gary and Richard are amazed and saddened that passers-by no longer ask to buy their crabs, for cooking them at home is nothing to be scared of. A scant 15 minutes in salted boiling water, prise apart the upper and lower shells, crack the claws and tuck into the flaky white meat or, my favourite, the strong-tasting brown meat that is the as yet unformed shell material. A bit of mayo, lemon juice and black pepper – heavenly. Alternately, try these recipes I have created for something a bit different.

This is one of the best ways of cooking and eating crab. Writers and chefs will be up in arms about my use of a shop-bought mayonnaise, with some justification. Home-made mayonnaise with brilliant yellow, free-range eggs, sea salt, extra virgin olive oil, cut with grapeseed oil, is one of life's great joys, but a lot of people find it too strong. The best way to cook crabs, and lobsters for that matter, is to boil water, salt and vinegar, then plunge in the crabs or lobsters, simmer for 5 minutes only, and turn off the heat. The residual heat will cook them perfectly. Leave to cool and chill completely in the liquor, which is the most important part. This will ensure a perfectly cooked crustacean every time.

BOILED CRAB
WITH MAYONNAISE

Serves: 4

2 live crabs, approx. 500g (18oz) each

water

white wine vinegar

salt

To serve

1 jar mayonnaise

juice of 1 lemon

2 tsp cracked black pepper

2 lemons, cut into wedges

2 little gem lettuces, washed well and quartered

1 Place the live crabs into the freezer for 2 hours so they relax.

2 Meanwhile boil a large pan of water that will hold both crabs, then add some vinegar and a good slug of sea salt, and bring back to the boil. (If you have, say, 2.2 litres/4 pints water, add 600ml/1 pint vinegar and 2 tbsp salt.) Pop in the crabs and simmer for 5 minutes, turn off the heat and cool, then chill well in the water.

3 Meanwhile mix the mayonnaise with the lemon juice and black pepper.

4 Pull off the top shell, leaving the legs and under-shell intact. Remove all the brown meat and keep separate. (This can be eaten at another time mixed with a few breadcrumbs and a little black pepper and salt added.) Carefully remove all the white meat from the carcass and gently crack the claws, leaving half the shell on. This is a bit of a pain, but well worth it.

5 Serve the white meat with the claws, mayonnaise, and lemon and lettuce wedges.

GT. YARMO

CROMER CRAB AND SWEETCORN RAMEKINS WITH MELBA TOASTS

Serves: 4

25g (1oz) unsalted butter

25g (1oz) plain flour

225ml (8fl oz) milk

1 tbsp vegetable oil

1 small onion, peeled and chopped

1 small garlic clove, peeled and crushed

2 tsp chopped tarragon

a pinch of chilli powder

2 x 170g (6oz) cans white crabmeat, drained

1 x 165g (6oz) can sweetcorn, drained

1 tsp anchovy essence (optional)

salt and freshly ground black pepper

55-115g (2–4oz) Gruyere cheese, grated

Melba toast
8 medium slices white bread

I know crab is quite expensive, but you can use canned white crabmeat. Of course fresh crab is preferable, but it can be difficult to get hold of and an almighty job to pick the meat out of the blighter! This is a really tasty dish, which can also be eaten cold on crackers – especially if they're spread with a little sweet chilli jam.

1 First make the white sauce. Melt the butter in a pan, then add the flour and stir in well. Gradually add the milk and stir over a moderate heat until the sauce thickens. Take the pan off the heat and allow to stand for 5 minutes.

2 Meanwhile, heat the oil in a frying pan. Add the onion and garlic and cook over a low heat until softened but not browned. Then add the tarragon and chilli powder and stir in.

3 Squeeze any excess liquid out of the crabmeat. Add the meat to the white sauce with the sweetcorn, onion mixture and anchovy essence (if using) and season. Spoon the mixture into four 7.5cm (3in) ramekins and leave to cool.

4 Meanwhile, toast the bread under a preheated grill on both sides until golden brown. Cut off the crusts then, using a bread knife, cut horizontally through each slice of toast to give two thin pieces. Cool slightly, then rub the uncooked sides of the toast together to remove any doughy, soggy crumbs.

5 Cut each slice in half diagonally. Reduce the heat of the grill, then toast the uncooked sides of the bread until golden, crispy and crunchy; seconds only.

6 Preheat the oven to 200°C/400°F/Gas 6.

7 Sprinkle the grated cheese over the crab mixture in the ramekins and cook in the oven for about 15 minutes, or until heated through and the cheese has melted. Serve straightaway with the Melba toast.

CROMER CRAB TART, WITH GREEN SALAD AND HOLLANDAISE

Serves: 6-8

1 x blind-baked shortcrust pastry flan or tart case, 25cm (10in) diameter and 4cm (1½in) deep (see page 17)

Filling

275ml (8½fl oz) brown crabmeat

1 garlic clove, peeled and chopped

2 pinches Madras curry powder

2 pinches saffron powder

1 pinch saffron stamens

100ml (3½fl oz) strong fresh crab stock

2 medium egg yolks

2 medium eggs

275ml (8½fl oz) whipping cream

salt and freshly ground black pepper

4 ripe tomatoes, skinned, seeded and cut into perfect cubes

4 tbsp finely chopped chives

225g (8oz) white crabmeat

Salad and dressing

1 head curly endive

2 bunches watercress

2 tsp Dijon mustard

3–4 tbsp sherry vinegar

a pinch of caster sugar

4 tbsp extra virgin olive oil

2 tbsp sunflower oil

Hollandaise sauce

4 tbsp white wine vinegar

4 tbsp cold water

1 shallot, peeled and finely sliced

a few celery leaves

a few crushed white peppercorns

4 large egg yolks, at room temperature

approx. 150g (5½oz) unsalted butter, melted and hot

a squeeze of lemon juice

This is such a nice combination. I have cooked this tart many times and it's still one of my favourites. Fresh white and brown crabmeat is best, but canned white meat and frozen brown are pretty good substitutes. Steer clear of frozen white crabmeat, as it's not very good. The addition of curry and saffron adds a nice, spicy edge to the whole flan, and cuts the richness of the crab custard. Try to roll the pastry as thinly as you can before blind-baking.

1 Preheat the oven to 220°C/425°F/Gas 7.

2 To make a 'crab cream' as the basis of the filling, place the brown crabmeat, garlic, curry powder, saffron powder and stamens and crab stock into a liquidizer and blitz until smooth. Spoon into a bowl, then whisk in the egg yolks, eggs and cream. Season well with salt and black pepper. Keep to one side.

3 Make the dressing for the salad leaves by placing the Dijon mustard, sherry vinegar and sugar into a bowl along with a pinch of salt and a little pepper. Gradually add the oils until you have a thick, semi-homogenized dressing.

4 Place the baked tart case on to a baking sheet and fill with tomato cubes, the chives and the white crabmeat. Spoon in the crab cream, place the tray in the oven and cook for 15 minutes, or until half set. Do not overcook. At this point remove from the oven and leave in a warm place to finish off the cooking. Preheat the grill.

5 For the hollandaise sauce, place the vinegar, 4 tbsp water, shallot, celery and peppercorns into a saucepan, bring to the boil and reduce by two-thirds.

6 In a bowl, start whisking the egg yolks and strain on to this the hot vinegar mixture, then whisk quickly over a pan of simmering water until very thick and foamy. Once cooked and thick gradually add the melted, hot butter until light and fluffy. Season well with salt and lemon juice.

7 To serve, spoon the hollandaise evenly over the tart, leaving it proud and full. Place under a hot grill to brown evenly; do not burn.

8 Place on a hot plate, and cut into wedges. Place the watercress and endive into a bowl, drizzle over a little dressing and season well.

ROCK
DOCWRAS ROCK

The day I finally went to Docwras was the adulthood realization of a childhood ambition. For years I'd wanted to revisit the amazing spectacle that is the making of seaside rock.

As a child, I spent many a happy, dentist-defying day munching my way through humbugs, sherbet pips, lemon bonbons, Pontefract cakes and the classic stick of rock. In part, this investment of my pocket money was a geographical inevitability. In Folkestone, where I grew up, was the acme of all rock shops, where you could watch rock being made for hours, not to mention a kaleidoscopic array of other traditional sweets.

Regent Road, Great Yarmouth, has been the home of the Docwra family's rock shop for 100 years, and it is the uncontested 'biggest rock shop in the world'. On my arrival I was greeted by the affable owner, Stephen Docwra, and also met Roy, master rock-maker for over 40 years.

Rock's raw materials are nothing more than sugar, glucose and an anti-foaming agent. Once the huge copper vat of sweetness comes to the right temperature, Roy and his assistant removed it from the heat and pour a torrent of liquid gold on to a special table with raised edges, to both cool it and begin the skilled process of manipulation. This is a dangerous procedure, molten sugar having a napalm-like ability to burn human skin. As the sugar cools, edible food dyes of red, yellow and blue are added for the external casing. These are stirred in roughly, creating overlapping rainbow swathes of colour. Next, with the sugar stiffening noticeably, Roy and his mate cut it into chunks with large scissors.

Now for the core. Some of the sugar and glucose mix has been kept to one side, and has cooled enough to be manually draped on to a three-pronged machine after being flavoured. This machine contra-rotates, pulling, stretching and folding the sugar in on itself. As the mixture cools and is worked, the 'mass' gains a white sheen, the result of air being trapped and folded through the sugar.

No stick of rock would be complete without the famous lettering. This is created by using rectangular bars of a dark red 'mass', assembled so the ends of the slabs form the letters, the whole assembly stretching off for 60-90cm (2-3 feet). They are finally surrounded by more white aerated mass.

With the coloured skin, the chewy core and the letters made, Roy and I construct them into one huge stubby stick of rock as big as a rolled-up duvet. This needs carrying towards a special rolling machine, and boy, does its weight catch you out as you roll it off the cooling table.

The rolling machine consists of two heated rollers which knead the huge stick of rock, thinning it from a diameter of about 60cm (2 feet), pushing it out the far end of the rollers, where it emerges on to the rolling table to a regulation 2cm (¾in) in diameter.

Pulled and shaped, it's amazing how many sticks of rock can come from the huge original. Within minutes, the rolling table had five or six lengths of rainbow-coloured sugar, each stick maybe 3 metres (10 feet) in length. Left to its own devices, the rock would flatten, so the ladies of Docwra have to roll these huge lengths until they cool and harden. After cutting, the rock is then wrapped in cellophane.

I wondered aloud, in this day and age of everything being bad for you, whether boiled sugar sweets like rock are still selling well. I was relieved to be told by Stephen Docwra, who'd inherited the business from his grandfather, that yes, the business has slowed but is still thriving.

SPEARMINT AND CHOCOLATE CHIP ROCK PARFAIT

Serves: 4-6

100g (3½g) bitter chocolate, roughly chopped

150g (5½oz or 2¼ sticks)

Docwra's spearmint rock, roughly chopped

250g (9oz) unrefined golden caster sugar

150ml (5fl oz) cold water

8 medium egg yolks

peppermint essence

600ml (1 pint) double cream, very lightly whipped

I have never written a recipe for rock before, so it was a challenge. By its very nature, it's a hard thing to cook with, but I think I have cracked this one. The burst of peppermint flavour, coupled with the crunchiness of the rock, makes a good fun pudding. The rock will break down over a week or so in the freezer, so eat it soon after it's frozen.

1 First melt the chocolate, then spread it on a board lined with a piece of baking parchment and leave to chill. When set, chop it up into small pieces.

2 Blitz 100g (3½oz) of the rock in a food processor, but not too finely. Remove and set aside.

3 Place the caster sugar and water in a pan and bring to the boil. Once boiling, leave to boil for 5 minutes, bang on, no more, no less. I use a small digital timer.

4 Place the egg yolks into a Kenwood mixer (see Note), and once the sugar and water have been boiling for 2 minutes, set the machine to medium speed.

5 At 5 minutes, take the sugar and water off the stove, turn the machine up to full speed, and carefully pour the syrup on to the egg yolks. Whisk until thick, foamy and cold, about 10 minutes. Remove the egg yolk mixture from the machine into a bowl, and scrape the last drops off the whisk.

6 Add the blitzed rock and the chocolate chips to the mixture and fold in a few drops of peppermint essence, taste it and mix well. Add the lightly whipped cream, pour into a plastic container, and then freeze overnight.

7 Serve scooped out into glasses. Break up the remaining rock with a sharp knife, and sprinkle over the parfait.

Note
A Kenwood mixer is best to use for the texture of this recipe, but you could use a food processor. It takes longer to whip up and to cool the mixture, and it will not thicken so well.

CHOCOLATE PEANUT BUTTER CHEESECAKE WITH MAPLE SYRUP

Serves: 8-10

Base

55g (2oz) unsalted butter

175g (6oz) digestive biscuits

25g (1oz) cocoa powder

Filling

400g (14oz) light cream cheese

115g (4oz) caster sugar

3 medium eggs

2 tbsp lemon juice

1¼ tsp pure vanilla extract

400ml (14fl oz) half-fat crème fraîche

70g (2½oz) smooth peanut butter, about 2 large tbsp

115g (4oz) plain chocolate, melted

To serve

4 tbsp maple syrup

This is a New York style cheese cake – smooth and perfectly creamy. You need to bake it the day before you want to eat it. Don't be tempted to skip the water in the roasting dish, or open the oven door... that's the secret for a successful texture.

1 Preheat the oven to 180°C/350°F/Gas 4. You will also need to grease and base-line a 20cm (8in) springform tin.

2 To make the base, melt the butter. Put the biscuits and cocoa powder into a food processor, blend until fine crumbs, and then combine with the butter mixture. Lightly press into the tin making an even layer. Chill.

3 For the filling, blend the cream cheese and sugar together in a food processor. Add the eggs, one at a time, with the processor running on low speed. Next add the lemon juice, vanilla and crème fraîche, blending until smooth.

4 Take the chilled biscuit base, and wrap the outside of the tin in a layer of clingfilm so that the base and the sides are watertight. Then repeat with tightly wrapped foil, for a double layer, and stand the tin in a roasting dish.

5 Pour half the cheesecake filling on to the biscuit base. Dot teaspoonfuls of peanut butter all over the batter, and then cover with the remainder of the cheesecake filling. Gently mix a thin stream of the melted chocolate into the batter, barely stirring, so that it ripples into the filling.

6 Surround the tin with 3cm (1¼in) boiling water from the kettle and bake in the centre of the oven for 45 minutes.

7 Turn off the oven and, without opening the door, leave the cheesecake in the oven for 1 hour to set. Remove and place on a rack to cool, then refrigerate overnight.

8 To serve, take the cheesecake out of the tin and put on a large plate. When you are ready to eat, pour the chilled maple syrup over the top of the cheesecake, criss-crossing to make a sticky glaze.

CUMBRIA AND THE NORTH-WEST

PORK
PETER GOTT
SILLFIELD FARM

Sillfield Farm is a real menagerie. Out in Peter Gott's 75 acres of fields are rare pig breeds such as Middle Whites, Saddlebacks and Tamworths, while in his 20 acres of traditional broad-leafed woodland you come face to face with the aptly named 'wild boar': straight out of the pages of Asterix and belligerent to the bone. There is also a breed unique to Sillfield Farm that Peter has dubbed 'Iron-Age' pigs, a cross created by breeding Tamworths with wild boar. The experiment has been a happy one. They have turned out a dead spit of the primitive, hardy porkers bred today in south-west Spain for the wonderful air-dried jamón serrano and iberico.

Rather than use the many dubious antibiotics and growth promoters that go hand in hand with so much modern pig husbandry, Peter lets nature take its course. Fed on a natural diet, even his fastest-maturing animals take a full eight months to grow, which gives their meat its deep flavour and fine texture. Peter lives, eats and breathes rare breeds and not just his own. He is full of interesting, if not downright depressing, facts: how we have lost 25 UK breeds to extinction in the past 30 years alone; how once upon a time nearly every county had its own local breed of pig (there are currently only 20 surviving Essex sows for instance – fewer even than there are giant pandas in the world).

I worked on farms as a teenager, have visited quite a few in my time and seldom have I seen such contented porkers as at Sillfield. They live a completely natural existence, foraging, playing and digging, which helps with the slow growth of the muscles and in particular produces the superb marbling of the animal's fat. The downside of Peter's passion is that, like all farmers, he is dealing with a cash crop not a farmful of pets. Peter does admit to sometimes shedding a tear when he has packed some of his favourites off to the slaughterhouse.

As well as his animals, I was delighted to see that Peter is passionate about sausage-making. He makes the best Cumberland sausage I have tasted – and I lived in Cumbria for five years. Peter is so proud of what he's got he told me he has petitioned Defra for a PDI (product designation indication) for Cumberland sausages. Just as Champagne can only come from a certain area and be made in a certain way, a PDI logo on your packet of bangers would tell you exactly what you were getting when you bought a Cumberland ring. If Peter gets his way, that would be a guaranteed minimum 90 per cent meat.

Peter is also making his own air-dried Cumberland hams and mutton. Trust me, these products rival almost anything I have tasted in Italy or Spain, despite him living in one of the wettest parts of the UK. One major fly-in-the-ointment is that whilst the Europeans air-dry their meats, Peter is having a real struggle to get permission to do the same thing here, even though air-drying was once commonplace in the UK.

Peter grew up on his mother's poultry farm, but his grandfather was a publican who farmed Cumberland pigs. Peter bought Sillfield Farm 21 years ago, and he is the first to admit that he made mistakes in the early days. In the last ten years, though, he has begun to produce champion food and now the farm employs 12 local people.

As well as the sausages and hams, let us not forget Sillfield's pies. Christine, Peter's wife, makes every one and very good they are too. The day I spent there, Christine cooked us a blow-out breakfast using the best of Peter's bacon and sausages, then promptly made 200 pies.

The traditional way of making hot-pot is to casserole scrag end of lamb with a potato crust in a pot packed full of root vegetables. Here there are a few changes, and I have added black pudding, honeyed pears and chickpeas: black pudding to give the whole dish a peppery bite and the pears for a sweet touch. I'm also using shoulder of pork instead of lamb neck. The shoulder has a nice amount of fat to keep the meat moist and tender. You can also add soaked pearl barley if you wish. My Mum still makes the best hot-pot, and this is based on her recipe.

PORK, HONEYED PEAR AND CHICKPEA HOT-POT

Serves: 4-6

4 tbsp vegetable oil

1 large carrot, peeled and chopped

2 small onions, peeled and chopped

2 large garlic cloves, peeled and crushed

2 level tbsp plain flour

1kg (2¼lb) shoulder of pork, skin removed, flesh cut into 5cm (2in) pieces

2 chicken stock cubes, crumbled into about 600ml (1 pint) boiling water

1 x 400g (14oz) can chickpeas, rinsed and drained well

salt and freshly ground black pepper

115g (4oz) good-quality black pudding, skinned and roughly chopped

finely grated zest of 1 lemon

4 baked honeyed pears, sliced

3 large baking potatoes, peeled and cut into 5mm (¼in) thick slices

lots of melted butter

1 Preheat the oven to 170°C/325°F/Gas 3.

2 Heat 3 tbsp of the vegetable oil in a sauté pan, add the carrot, onion and garlic, and cook over a medium heat until they have a nice colour and have wilted slightly. Add the flour and mix together.

3 In a separate pan, heat the remaining oil and brown the pieces of pork in batches if necessary. Transfer the browned meat to an ovenproof braising dish or shallow pan, and pour on enough stock to come halfway up the meat (this allows for extra moisture that will come from the vegetables and pork).

4 Sprinkle the chickpeas and the carrot, onion and garlic mixture over the top, and season well. Top with the black pudding, lemon zest and sliced cooked pears, then lay on the sliced potatoes, overlapping slightly. Season well and butter liberally.

5 Cover with tightly fitting foil then bake for about 1¼ hours.

6 Remove the foil, butter the potatoes again and place back into the oven for a further 45-60 minutes to brown up the potatoes. You may need to turn the temperature up to slightly crisp them.

7 This dish is best eaten when it has been left to cool for about half an hour or so, or it's too hot. I'm a great fan of pickled cabbage and it works perfectly with hot-pots or any braised meats. Just tuck in.

BAKED GAMMON AND BEETROOT WITH MARROW PICKLE

Serves: 4-6

8 small beetroots, the size of a satsuma

1 x 1.2kg (2½lb) gammon joint, skin on, soaked overnight and dried well

salt and freshly ground black pepper

extra virgin olive oil

Pickle

4 tbsp good-quality olive oil

1 tsp caraway seeds

1 tsp juniper seeds, crushed

1 tsp whole cloves

2 garlic cloves, peeled and crushed

1 tbsp finely chopped fresh root ginger

1 small red onion, peeled and finely chopped

1 small white onion, peeled and finely chopped

450g (1lb) marrow flesh, no skin or seeds

125ml (4fl oz) red wine vinegar

2 tbsp balsamic vinegar

1 tbsp Worcestershire sauce

175g (6oz) light brown muscovado sugar

This is an unusual way of cooking ham, and although it does take a bit of time, it is well worth the effort. Great eaten hot or cold for breakfast or brunch, which is when the Victorians liked to eat savoury compotes, relishes and pickles. I have cooked this pickle recipe for years and works really well with gammon or ham.

1 Preheat the oven to 200°C/400°F/Gas 6.

2 Top and tail the beetroots, then scrub clean under running cold water. Wrap each beet tightly in foil and place on to a baking tray. Bake for 45 minutes, or until soft when pierced with a knife or skewer. Leave to cool for 15 minutes, then unwrap, when the skin should come away easily. Keep to one side, covered.

3 Turn the temperature of the oven down to 170°C/325°F/Gas 3.

4 Place the gammon in a small baking tray. Sprinkle with a little black pepper, then cover tightly with two layers of foil. Bake for about 2¼-2½ hours.

5 Meanwhile get on with making the pickle. To start, heat the olive oil in a large pan. Add the caraway seeds, juniper berries, cloves, garlic and ginger, and cook for about 6-8 minutes – you'll get a wonderful smell all around the kitchen. Add the onions and marrow and stir in. Then add the vinegars, Worcestershire sauce and sugar, stir well and season with salt and pepper. Cook slowly until the marrow is tender, about 15 minutes; you will end up with an unctuous, deep-coloured mixture.

6 After 2¼ hours, check to see if the gammon is cooked. To test, remove the foil and insert a skewer through the centre of the gammon: there should be a little resistance, but not too firm, and a little juice should run out also. If slightly undercooked, then allow a further 15 minutes. Warm the beetroots through with the gammon for the last 30 minutes or so. Cut into quarters and drizzle with a little extra virgin olive oil and a little salt and pepper.

7 Slice the gammon in thick slices and serve with the pickle, roasted beets and perhaps a fried egg or two.

CUMBERLAND SAUSAGEMEAT AND LEEK PIE

Serves: 6-8

2 x 375g (13oz) packets ready-rolled shortcrust pastry

salt and freshly ground black pepper

a little beaten egg, to glaze

sesame seeds

Filling

3 medium leeks, split (but still attached at the base), and washed very well

700g (1lb 9oz) good-quality sausagemeat

½ tsp freshly ground black pepper

2 heaped tbsp roughly chopped basil

1 medium egg, beaten

My dear Mum used to make a version of this wonderful pie, so I sort of stole the idea from her. We used to eat it with warm new potatoes cooked in a little mint, and a green salad, always in the summer months when we came home from school. The best thing about this pie is that it can also be transported well, making it ideal for outdoor eating. Two things to remember: make sure you wash the leeks very well, or it's like eating sandwiches on the beach, and use good-quality sausagemeat. I have found that Peter Gott's Cumberland sausage, with its spicy edge, works really well in this pie.

1 Preheat the oven to 190°C/375°F/Gas 5.

2 Cut the pastry sheets into two discs, one of 35cm (14in) and the other of 24cm (9½in). Use the larger one to line a greased, loose-bottomed flan tin, 24cm (9½in) in diameter, and 4cm (1½in) deep. Push the pastry well into the base of the tin, and make sure the pastry hangs over the edge. Dock or prick well with a fork and chill.

3 Bring a large pan of water to the boil, add a little salt and plunge the leeks in. Cook for 3 minutes to soften, then refresh under cold water, drain well and lay on kitchen paper.

4 Place the sausagemeat in a bowl, add ½ tsp pepper, the basil and a little salt, and mix well. Add the whole beaten egg and mix well again.

5 Place half the sausagemeat into the prepared pastry case. Lay the leeks on top and season well. Top with the other half of the sausagemeat, then pack down well. Make sure the pie is over-full.

6 Moisten the edges of the pastry rim with a little beaten egg. Lay over the other disc of pastry and seal well. Trim off any excess, then crimp the edges. Brush with beaten egg to glaze, and sprinkle over some sesame seeds. Make three incisions in the lid.

7 Bake for 25-30 minutes, or until light golden in colour. Remove from the oven and leave to cool. Chill well, best overnight, before cutting and eating.

8 Serve with a ripe tomato and onion salad, at room temperature, dressed with a little sherry vinegar and extra virgin olive oil.

PIGS' TROTTERS WITH FIVE-SPICE AND HONEY GLAZE

Serves: 2

4 pigs' trotters, cleaned and washed

1 onion

2 celery stalks

2 carrots

salt and freshly ground black pepper

a few whole black peppercorns

3 chicken stock cubes

2 star anise

1 tsp Chinese five-spice powder

2 bay leaves

Glaze

4 tsp Chinese five-spice powder

8 tbsp runny honey

8 tbsp sherry vinegar

4 garlic cloves, peeled and very finely chopped

2 tbsp tomato purée

300ml (10fl oz) full-bodied red wine

150ml (5fl oz) olive oil

If you like trotters, then you will adore this recipe. If not, then please try it: the jelly-like texture is delicious. As a child we had trotters fairly often, as my father adored them: boiled, cooled and eaten with pickled onions was the norm. My father (along with my late grandfather) loved all sorts of unusual foods, and I can remember him eating tripe, boiled cow heels (Desperate Dan style), trotters and 'wassle' (a Lancashire word for boiled cow's udder). All these he ate mostly when we were on our annual trip to Blackpool, and were readily available from the tripe shop on Abingdon Street (now gone), with its red frontage and steep marble slabs. The trotters we had then were just plain boiled, but they do lend themselves to glazing with strong flavours. In northern Italy I had them recently at an outdoor evening food festival. They had been boiled then breadcrumbed with chilli, fried and served with a spicy salsa verde. They were delicious. I love the glutinous texture of trotters, real finger food!

1 Wrap the trotters very tightly in several layers of tin foil.

2 Place them into a large saucepan and add the vegetables, 2 pinches salt, the peppercorns, stock cubes, star anise, five-spice powder and bay. Cover with water and bring to the boil. Once boiling, taste the stock and adjust so it has a full flavour, almost too strong in salt, chicken and pepper.

3 Reduce the heat and gently simmer in an unlidded pan for about 2¼ hours, or until the trotters are soft and juicy. Top up the water level if necessary. The trotters may split slightly if cooked too quickly, but don't worry about this, it's normal when the tendons shrink.

4 Once cooked, cool in the stock and chill well, best overnight. The next day remove the trotters from the jelly and unwrap carefully.

5 Preheat the oven to 180°C/350°F/Gas 6.

6 Place the trotters in a baking tray or shallow saucepan. Place all the ingredients for the glaze into a bowl and mix well. Spoon the marinade over the cooked trotters and place in the oven. Cook for about 40 minutes, basting every 10 minutes or so, so the glaze sticks and colours. The sauce will thicken naturally and eventually self-glaze. But keep an eye on it.

7 Serve the trotters at room temperature, with a bowl of mash and some lightly boiled purple sprouting broccoli, or Geoffrey's clotted cream runner beans. The only way to eat them is just warm, with your fingers!

GRILLED CUMBERLAND SAUSAGE WITH STEVE'S TIKKA BEANS

Serves: 4

500g (18oz) Cumberland sausage

hot creamy mashed potatoes, to serve

Steve's tikka beans

4 tbsp sunflower or olive oil

25g (1oz) unsalted butter

1 tsp caster sugar

2 tsp each of garam masala and ground cumin

2 tsp coriander seeds, crushed

2 tsp ground fenugreek

½ small onion, peeled and very finely chopped

1 tbsp finely chopped fresh root ginger

2 garlic cloves, peeled and crushed

2 tbsp tikka paste

2 tbsp tomato purée

100ml (3½fl oz) tomato passata or tomato juice

200ml (7fl oz) chicken or veg stock

4 tbsp double cream

200g (7oz) well cooked haricot beans (I hate hard beans!)

2 tbsp chopped coriander

These are great beans, which have the wonderful flavour of the creamy chicken tikka masala we are all used to, but without the chicken. This recipe we hope will become a classic, as it combines many fantastic flavours such as coriander, tomatoes, ginger, onions, garlic, and ground spices such as cumin, coriander, fenugreek and garam masala, finished with a dash of double cream. Try and use canned haricot beans, which are pretty good for this sort of dish. Failing that you can rinse off a tin or two of baked beans, which work just as well; they're slightly softer and may break up a little. The beans are great over jacket potatoes as a supper dish, or poured over basmati rice with some brinjal pickle and mango chutney. Why not add some chicken to them and enjoy as a normal tikka masala: the beans are a great additional carbohydrate. If you want them hotter, try adding a few dried red chilli flakes to spice things up a bit. I like mine over hot buttered toast after playing football on a Wednesday night.

1 Heat the oil and butter in a large pan, then add the sugar and spices and cook for 2 minutes over a moderate heat to release their flavour and aroma. Do not burn. Add the onion, ginger and garlic, and cook for 5 minutes. Add the tikka paste and tomato purée and cook for 5 minutes. Add the passata, stock and cream and bring to the boil. Add the beans and fresh coriander, season with salt and pepper, and bring back to the boil. Cook until you have a nice thick sauce, probably about 10 minutes.

2 Grill or fry the sausage until cooked and nice and golden.

3 Serve the sausage with some mash, and a couple of spoonfuls of beans all over. That's it! Oh, by the way, the beans are great cold as a dip.

SHRIMPS
LES SALISBURY AT MORECAMBE BAY

Les Salisbury is something of a Lancashire institution, having been shrimping for the best part of half a century, man and boy, horse and tractor. His company is only one of a handful left still fishing the treacherous sands and galloping tides of Morecambe Bay in pursuit of the lovely little brown shrimps that are his livelihood.

I arranged to meet Les on an ebbing tide one cold September morning at 4.30. The sun was just clearing the distant Lakeland fells as we piled on to Les's (t)rusty tractor, while his fishing partners-in-crime, Eric and Billy, fired up another each, and we zoomed off like decrepit Thunderbirds. These fine machines are for running in quite deep seawater, with big mudguards to keep the bow-wave from engulfing the driver.

With the saltwater still heading out to sea, so did we, to give us maximum safe time out in the bay. A couple of miles out, the trailer carrying Les's finely meshed nets starts work. (These trailers started life as cars before having all the bodywork stripped out.) The ancient steering wheel's put on full lock and lashed in place. The nets are set up, sticking out either side of the trailer, then Les lets out yards of towrope. As the tractor gains speed, the trailer obeys the steering wheel and veers off to one side and into a gully or 'dyke' containing deeper water. Les and his boys patrol their tractors up and down safely in the shallows while the robotic trailers all but disappear into the depths.

After a couple of passes, the tractors all park up in a huddle to process their catch. The nets are emptied and the contents are gone through: 'riddled' is the technical term. The haul gave you a real snapshot of what was out there: plaice, assorted small-fry, angry-looking crabs and of course lots of lovely shrimps. There are still rich pickings out there – two tractor passes netted about 40kg (90lb) of shrimps.

After an hour of this trawling, we were some three miles from shore. Uppermost in my mind was the fate of 23 Chinese cockle-pickers who'd died out here only a few months before; they'd been caught out too far to outrun the incoming tide and drowned. Les's lifelong experience and respect for these fast-moving tides help to keep him and his team safe; he told me not to

September – Tractors took us one and a half miles across the sand to fish for shrimps from the beach on a late summer's day

worry, as we had three tractors to keep an eye on each other. If one does get stuck, Les and his lads abandon the tractor out in the bay, and come back the next day to re-float it on the next high tide.

Once back on dry land with our catch we headed to the Ulverston home of Les's mate Ray, who is a guide, appointed by the Queen, to take walkers across the dangerous sands of Morecambe Bay. Here we unloaded the shrimps for boiling and hand-picking. Les also runs clever machines that use pinpoint water jets to blast the shells off – which, says Les, become worn out by the constant diet of sand and are still slower than the ladies he employs to hand-peel the shrimps in the traditional way of fishermen's wives. I joined the ladies at their table, grabbed a pint of shrimps and tried – and failed – to keep up with them!

Once boiled, cleaned and shelled, the shrimps get boiled in butter and spices (to a secret recipe by Les's nephew) and are then poured into traditional ramekins. They are topped with melted butter, left to cool and sent to the supermarkets and even sold at London's foodie heaven, Borough Market.

I think that if people knew how much love and work goes into such an apparently small-scale product, then they would never query the price.

POTTED SHRIMPS

Serves: 6

8 shallots, peeled and finely chopped

2 garlic cloves, peeled and crushed

55g (2oz) unsalted butter

50ml (2fl oz) olive oil

100g (3½oz) shelled shrimps

200g (7oz) brown Morecambe Bay shrimps

finely grated zest and juice of ½ lemon

2 tsp freshly grated nutmeg, to taste

2 tsp powdered mace, to taste

a small pinch of cayenne pepper

salt and freshly ground black pepper

Clarified butter

200g (7oz) unsalted butter

This is an absolute classic and needs very little introduction. Just warm slightly and serve on thick toast. I can still remember the sweet smell when we cooked these in Cumbria with Les Salisbury, lovely.

1 Cook the shallot and garlic together until soft in the butter and olive oil, about 10 minutes, then cool slightly.

2 Melt the butter for clarifying very slowly so you end up with curds and whey, clear on the top, cloudy at the base. Leave to settle.

3 Tip into a large bowl along with the cooled shallot mixture, the shrimps, lemon juice and zest, and the spices and stir well. Season with salt and pepper; I would slightly over-season at this point because you are going to add a fair amount of unsalted butter.

4 Pour half the clarified melted butter into the bowl with the shallot mixture and prawns and stir well, trying to keep as much of the buttermilk as possible in the pan. Spoon the buttery mixture into six small ramekins, and chill well for a minimum of 4 hours.

5 Top with the remaining clarified butter, again keeping as much of the buttermilk as possible in the pan.

6 When ready to eat, remove the potted shrimps from the fridge 1 hour in advance of eating or pop the bowl in the microwave on defrost and just soften for 1 minute. Serve with char-grilled sourdough bread, some watercress and avocado slices drizzled with olive oil and fresh lime juice.

BROWN SHRIMP PIL-PIL

Andy, who used to work for me, devised this recipe, and I loved it. It was a big seller when we had the pub, and the whole place had a wonderful aroma when it was served. The sauce is thick, oily and semi-split, which is exactly how it should be, so don't panic. Shell-on raw freshwater or defrosted cooked Atlantic prawns also work well in this dish if you like getting messy.

Serves: 2

4 tbsp olive oil

1 small red onion, peeled and finely chopped

4 garlic cloves, peeled and finely chopped

2 tbsp palm sugar

1 tbsp smoked paprika

3 tbsp fresh lime juice (about 2 limes)

2 pinches dried red chilli flakes

salt and freshly ground black pepper

175g (6oz) brown Morecambe Bay shrimps
or small prawns

1 Heat the oil in a frying pan, add the onion and garlic and cook for 5 minutes to soften. Add the palm sugar, paprika, lime juice and chilli flakes and cook for 15 minutes over a very low heat to thicken. Season well with salt and pepper. The sauce is quite thick and oily, which is intentional. It's best if you can leave this for a day or so in the fridge to enhance and intensify the flavours.

2 To serve, gently heat the sauce then drop in the shrimps and cook through. Do not overcook.

3 Serve with steamed rice and a few fresh peas or runner beans.

CREAMED SHRIMPS

This recipe I picked up in 1980 when I was cooking at a hotel in the Lakes. It's fairly dated now, but it really brings out the flavour of the shrimps.

Serves: 4

35g (1¼oz) unsalted butter

35g (1¼oz) plain flour

250ml (9fl oz) warm milk

2 tbsp olive oil

1 small onion, peeled and finely chopped

150ml (5fl oz) medium white wine

350g (12oz) brown shrimps

100ml (3½fl oz) double cream

2 tsp Tabasco sauce

4 tsp Worcestershire sauce

salt and freshly ground black pepper

a pinch of fish stock cube

55g (2oz) Parmesan, grated (optional)

4 tbsp roughly chopped parsley

1 Melt the butter in a saucepan, then mix in the flour. Cook over a low heat for 2-3 minutes. Do not burn. Gradually add the warm milk and stir over a medium heat, then slowly increase the heat and stir to the boil. Cook for 1 minute, then cool slightly.

2 Meanwhile, pour the olive oil into a separate pan over a moderate heat. Add the onion and cook for 3-4 minutes. Add the white wine, bring to the boil, then simmer until almost all the wine is gone.

3 Add the white sauce to the onions and mix well. Add all of the remaining ingredients, then taste and season again if necessary.

4 To serve, warm through, (do not over-heat) and serve with Melba toast and a watercress salad.

GRILLED PLAICE WITH CURRIED SHRIMP AND WATERCRESS BUTTER

Serves: 2

125g (4½oz) unsalted butter

2 whole plaice, roughly 550-600g (1lb 4-5oz) each, wings, skin and head removed (your fishmonger will do this for you)

salt and freshly ground black pepper

1-2 tsp good-quality curry paste, cooked (see above)

4 spring onions, roughly chopped on the diagonal

juice of 2 fresh limes

1 small bunch watercress, roughly chopped

100g (3½oz) shelled brown shrimps

I like to see whole fish cooked on the bone. It really makes a difference to the flavour and texture; a lot of the moisture is retained in the flakes. This dish works well with other whole fish such as Dover sole and lemon sole. Cooking off the curry paste ensures you don't get that raw, harsh spice flavour – just heat it for a few minutes in a small non-stick frying pan or saucepan.

1 Preheat the grill to its hottest setting.

2 Melt 25g (1oz) of the butter, and use some to grease a baking tray well. Lay the plaice on the tray, then butter the fish generously with more of the melted butter. Sprinkle with a little salt and pepper and place under the hot grill for about 15 minutes, turning once.

3 Meanwhile, heat the remaining butter until it starts to foam and turn slightly brown (this is called '*noisette*' butter), then add the cooked curry paste off the heat. Immediately add the spring onions and lime juice, stir well, then season. Finally, add the chopped watercress and shrimps and wilt slightly. Do not overheat or the watercress will turn a horrible olive-green colour.

4 Check to see if the fish are cooked by pressing gently – there should be a little resistance. Do not overcook.

5 To serve, carefully lift the plaice off the tray and place on warm serving plates. Spoon over the watercress and shrimp butter. Serve with boiled new potatoes and a few mixed vegetables.

SHRIMP SALAD WITH ROAST VEGETABLES

Serves: 4

2 tbsp sherry vinegar

salt and freshly ground black pepper

½ head iceberg lettuce, roughly chopped

225g (8oz) brown shrimps

3 pickled walnuts, roughly chopped

Roast vegetables

1 x 250g (9oz) bunch carrots

250g (9oz) small courgettes

2 Romano peppers

1 medium aubergine

4 garlic cloves, cut in half, skins on

approx. 6 tbsp good-quality olive oil

I really like vegetable salads, especially in the summer months; it's the best time to eat bunched carrots, courgettes, aubergines, fresh peas and broad beans. I am a great believer that the simpler the better, and get quite nervous eating in restaurants when I see dishes like broad bean purée or asparagus tip purée. Really, what's the point when you have a perfect vegetable, like a gorgeous spear of asparagus, or a perfect baby carrot beautifully fresh, and as sweet as possible? All these need is a little salt, freshly ground pepper and maybe some butter or good olive oil to help them on their way. With this in mind I have tried to match a few old masters together: subtly flavoured shrimps, pickled walnuts with their sweet treacly edge, and perfect roasted summer vegetables. The dressing is just the olive oil the vegetables were cooked in plus a little sherry vinegar.

1 Preheat the oven to 220°C/425°F/Gas 7. Wash all the vegetables well in cold water and dry well with kitchen paper.

2 Leave the carrots and courgettes whole; slice the peppers in half lengthwise and remove all the seeds. Trim the aubergine and slice lengthwise into 2cm (¾in) batons.

3 Place the vegetables and garlic in a large roasting tray and drizzle over the olive oil and salt and pepper. Mix well with your hands. Cover with foil, roast until nice and soft. This will take about 40-50 minutes. When cooked, strain off the oil (retain this) and let the vegetables cool to room temperature.

4 To finish, place all the vegetables into a large bowl. Pour over 4 tbsp of the olive oil used for cooking plus the sherry vinegar and season with a little salt and pepper. Mix well. Carefully add the chopped lettuce, shrimps and pickled walnuts, then lightly mix. Do not over-work the leaves or they will wilt very quickly.

5 Place on a large serving plate, pop in the middle of the table and let everybody tuck in. Just serve with plenty of crusty bread. The secret to this salad is to have everything at room temperature and to try and get a good balance of flavours, textures and tastes A great starter or summer main course.

GINGERBREAD
GRASMERE GINGERBREAD

For me, going back to Grasmere in the Lake District was a real trip back in time. I'd lived there as a young chef, cutting my teeth – and so much else besides – in one of the village hotels. Besieged by tourists by the coach-load in the summer and hemmed in by weather and mist-covered mountains in the winter, I thought I'd really exhausted the village's possibilities in the five years that I lived there. But there was one village institution that astoundingly, incomprehensibly, I had never once visited: Sarah Nelson's Grasmere Gingerbread shop.

Today, 15 years on, the tiny bakery and gingerbread shop is a real magnet for me and all those tourists who always knew better than I. The building used to be the village school with a minor, little-remembered poet called Wordsworth its teacher. When I visited, the Sarah Nelson advertised on the shop sign outside is nowhere to be seen. She started the gingerbread business in 1854 and long ago hung up her apron. Today the business is run by Andrew Wilson and his wife Joanne, who serves behind the counter in a traditional voluminous Victorian costume so suited to this charmingly traditional shop.

There are beautifully wrapped parcels of gingerbread all around. It's almost inconceivable that so much produce comes out of so tiny a kitchen. Well, I imagine from the size of the building that the kitchen's tiny. I was expressly forbidden more than a momentary glimpse of it, so secret is the Wilsons' gingerbread recipe. Even Joanne doesn't know what goes into the golden slabs she helps produce and sell. On the day I visited, Andrew good-naturedly batted away all my requests for the recipe, revealing only that the family recipe is known to him and one other and is locked away in a bank vault. Andrew pulled my leg by saying that even if I had the recipe I wouldn't be able to reproduce gingerbread as good as his. He may well be right an' all!

If you've ever bought a packet of ginger nuts or even a hand-made gingerbread man from a bakery elsewhere, don't think you know about gingerbread until you've tried this stuff. It's buttery, moist, deliciously chewy with – of course – fabulous hints of exotic spice. Nearby Kendal can keep its mint cake, this stuff is divine.

This pudding is a bit like a crème brûlée, but the crunchy topping is far nicer than a thick layer of sugar, in my opinion.

BAKED HONEY CREAM WITH SPICED GINGERBREAD TOPPING

Serves: 6-8

6 medium egg yolks

65g (2¾oz) runny honey

600ml (1 pint) whipping cream

2 pinches ground allspice

1 vanilla pod, split

Topping

55g (2oz) caster sugar

200g (7oz) Grasmere gingerbread, finely crumbled

¼ tsp ground cinnamon

¼ tsp freshly grated nutmeg

a pinch of ground allspice

1 Preheat the oven to 140°C/275°F/Gas 1. Lightly grease a 24cm (9½in) square, 4cm (1½in) deep, baking dish.

2 Place the egg yolks and honey in a bowl and gently mix together.

3 Meanwhile place the cream, allspice and vanilla pod in a pan and slowly bring to the boil. Once boiling, pour on to the beaten egg yolks and honey, whisk together well, then leave to cool and infuse for 10 minutes.

4 Strain the mixture through a sieve, then pour into the prepared serving dish. Carefully place in a deep baking tray, and pour boiling water from a kettle into the tray until the water is halfway up the side of the dish. Cover the whole tray lightly with foil and bake for 30 minutes, or until just set. Remember, the residual heat in the custard will carry on the cooking process for a good 10 minutes or so once it has been removed from the oven.

5 Remove from the oven and leave to cool, then chill well.

6 Meanwhile, mix the sugar, gingerbread crumbs and spices together, and gently warm under a grill. Do not burn, just toast lightly, then cool.

7 To serve, remove the dish from the fridge, then top generously with the toasted gingerbread.

GINGERBREAD AND LIME SOUFFLÉ

Serves: 4

3 tsp arrowroot

finely grated zest and juice of 3 large unwaxed limes

115g (4oz) caster sugar

60g (2¼oz) unsalted butter

4 medium eggs, separated, at room temperature

3-4 tbsp lime or lemon curd

a pinch of cream of tartar

40g (1½oz) icing sugar

100g (3½oz) Grasmere gingerbread, very finely crumbled (in the food processor)

This is a quick and fairly simple pudding. You don't have to worry about it rising too much, because you are 'setting' it, rather than wanting it to rise perfectly. It's nice eaten hot or cold. The real secret is not to over-whip the whites or the pudding will be too firm.

1 Preheat the oven to 200°C/400°F/Gas 6. You will need a baking dish, either oval, 24 x 7.5cm (9 x 3in), or an 18cm (7in) round soufflé dish.

2 Mix the arrowroot to a paste with a little of the lime juice. Place the rest of the juice, the zest and 70g (2½oz) of the caster sugar in a small pan and bring to a gentle simmer. Stir in the arrowroot, and cook for 1 minute, until nicely thickened. Whisk in the butter, and then remove from the heat and leave to cool slightly. Add the egg yolks and stir well.

3 Spoon the lemon or lime curd into the bottom of the baking dish, and spread out evenly.

4 Pop the egg whites into a mixing bowl with the cream of tartar and whisk until they are thick and foamy, at not too high a speed. If you whisk too quickly the meringue will be too tight and the soufflé will not rise and will become hard. Add the remaining caster sugar and whisk until the egg whites are at soft peak, not too stiff. Finally whisk in the icing sugar; again don't go mad.

5 Remove the bowl from the machine and fold the gingerbread crumbs gently through the mixture.

6 Place the cooked juice, egg yolk and butter mixture into a large mixing bowl, add half the egg white, and whisk well. Then add the rest of the whites, folding in carefully.

7 Spoon into the baking dish and pop into the oven. Cook until nicely browned and slightly risen, about 15 minutes. The secret to this pudding is to make sure that the middle is soft and the outside is nice and brown.

8 Dust with a little extra icing sugar and serve with double cream.

CLEMENTINE AND GINGERBREAD UPSIDE-DOWN PUDDING

Serves: 6-8

55g (2oz) caster sugar

6 clementines, peeled, left whole

Batter

3 medium eggs

100g (3½oz) caster sugar

150g (5½oz) Grasmere gingerbread, finely chopped

50ml (2fl oz) milk

finely grated zest of 1 large unwaxed lemon

2 pinches salt

125g (4½oz) self-raising flour

125g (4½oz) unsalted butter, melted

Syrup

juice of 3 large lemons

115g (4oz) icing sugar

This recipe doubles up quite nicely. On one hand you have a hot sponge pudding, that only needs plenty of custard poured over. On the other hand you have a cold, moist cake that is really nice to eat with thick or clotted cream, or even ice-cream. The gingerbread gives the sponge a nice spicy edge. This recipe is really easy and, from start to finish, will only take 40 minutes.

1 Preheat the oven to 200°C/400°F/Gas 6.

2 Place the sugar in a non-stick frying pan, about 28cm (11in) in diameter and 4cm (1½in) deep, and melt over a low heat, until you have a light caramel. Cut the clementines in half, and place carefully, uncut-side down, into the hot caramel.

3 For the batter, place the eggs, sugar, Grasmere gingerbread, milk, lemon zest and salt together in a bowl, and whisk well. Add the flour and then the melted butter and mix well. Pour the batter over the bubbling caramel and clementines.

4 Bake for 25-30 minutes on a low heat until light golden-brown and well risen. Turn out immediately.

5 To make the syrup, boil the lemon juice and sugar together for 1 minute.

6 Pour over the cake when still warm.

7 Eat hot with custard or cold as an upside-down cake with thick pouring cream.

MARMALADE
DUERR'S

There can be few images that say 'thriving Northern factory' better than the view on first arriving in the back streets of Old Trafford, Manchester. Stretching off into the distance were rows of back-to-back houses just like on the *Coronation Street* titles. Perfectly framed at the end of the lane was Duerr's factory, shrouded in billowing clouds of steam.

F. Duerr & Sons specialize in jars of fine and chunky-cut marmalade, jams of many different varieties and peanut butters, having been in the preserves business since 1881. The company boardroom is full of fascinating photos of old production processes and workers dating back many years. Duerr's carefully preserved records of all the old packaging and adverts make a fascinating history of the company's fortunes.

These days Duerr's is run by two brothers, Mark and Richard, who inherited the business from their father some years ago. The boys are a great double act, with their perfectly matched, dry Mancunian wit, and have a great future on stage should running a multi-million pound business ever prove lacking in excitement.

The history of this great business makes fascinating reading. It began with housewife Mary Duerr (Mark and Richard's great-great-grandmother) hand-making small batches of jam and marmalade in her Manchester home and selling the surplus to friends and neighbours and then to a local store. That business grew and grew from a scullery operation to the large-volume producer it is today.

Even now, all of Duerr's marmalade oranges come from Seville as tradition dictates. They are small and sour, and luckily for the Duerr family, the Spanish don't make much marmalade and have never seen the point in keeping all these tart little greeny-orange fruits for themselves. Where once they were shipped whole

and minced up in-house, these days they come ready shredded and are delivered to Manchester in large blue plastic drums. The Duerrs buy the entire output of many southern Spanish orange-growers, a whopping 1,680 tons every year.

Once in Duerr's factory the orange chunks are tipped into huge stainless-steel vats, where they are mixed with sugar, the setting agent pectin and water and are simply boiled to make the marmalade 'jam'. It sounds easy, doesn't it, but it's a very carefully worked-out process, carried out by real masters of the craft.

Originally in the Old Trafford factory, as the photos in the boardroom show, all of Duerr's marmalades and jams were made by hand, boiled up over naked flames and stirred and carried about in huge open copper pans. All this boiling water and molten sugar made for an extremely dangerous process and very hard work. These days, the preserve-making processes are all hidden away in stainless-steel vats and pipework, the activity betrayed only by noise, heat and steam. This original factory, now fully automated and computerized, is still working flat out to produce a wonderful list of great British favourites, from redcurrant jelly to grapefruit and thick-cut marmalades. All of it is overseen by the factory manager, Vivanne.

Coming at the end of the preserve-making process, the bottling plant was a fascinating Wonka-esque place, with jars whizzing about on conveyor belts all over the place, at all heights and angles. Keen to see the lids going on the marmalade and being naturally nosy, I opened the lid of a hopper. Little did I realize the lid was linked to a safety trip-switch that shut off this section of the process. Within seconds jars were backing up, and there was the crash of breaking glass all over the building. All told, I made them lose some 35 jars that day. Mark will never let me forget it, and I'm just waiting for the bill.

ERR'S

1881

TURKEY ESCALOPES WITH CHERRY AND MARMALADE RELISH

Serves: 4

Turkey escalopes

a dash of milk

2 medium eggs, lightly beaten

4 x 125g (4½oz) turkey breast escalopes

2 tbsp plain flour

200g (7oz) dried breadcrumbs

2 tbsp olive oil

25g (1oz) unsalted butter

salt and freshly ground black pepper

Cherry and bitter marmalade relish

1 tbsp olive oil

2 tsp ground cumin

1 tsp caraway seeds

2 small red onions, peeled and very finely chopped

3 garlic cloves, peeled and crushed

200g (7oz) semi-dried, stoned cherries

175g (6oz) thick-cut marmalade

100ml (3½fl oz) dry white wine

200ml (7fl oz) water

75ml (2½fl oz) cider vinegar

1 tbsp chopped fresh root ginger

salt and freshly ground black pepper

4 tbsp extra virgin olive oil

Turkey is much underused in Britain. Most of us only eat it once a year, apart from the occasional awful shaved turkey ham (whatever that is) sandwich. It takes great skill to get the best out of turkey, due to its very low fat content. I have spent many hours cooking turkey in all sorts of ways, but sometimes the old ways are the best. Cooking as escalopes keeps the turkey breast nice and moist, and served with the relish this makes a great supper or lunch dish.

1 Make the relish first. Heat the olive oil in a large pan, add the spices and cook for a few seconds to release their aromas. Do not allow to burn. Add all the remaining ingredients except the extra virgin olive oil. Stir well, bring to the boil and gently simmer until thick and pulpy. This will probably take about 25-30 minutes or so.

2 Stir in the extra virgin olive oil, then season again with salt and pepper, and cool. Place in a small bowl or large jar, seal well with clingfilm or a lid, and keep in the fridge (for a week or so).

3 To start the escalopes, mix the milk and the eggs together in a bowl. Season the turkey escalopes well, then dust in the flour. Dip one escalope at a time in the beaten egg and milk mixture, then coat in the breadcrumbs. Repeat with the remaining escalopes, then chill well.

4 Heat the oil and butter in a frying pan on a medium heat until just foaming. Add the escalopes and cook for about 5 minutes on each side, or until cooked through. They should be nicely browned and golden. Do not overcook.

5 Serve on warmed plates with a little buttered kale or cabbage and a large spoon of cherry and bitter marmalade relish.

STICKY MARMALADE CHICKEN THIGHS

Serves: 4

6 tbsp vegetable oil

8 chicken thighs, bone in, skin removed

1 small onion, peeled and very finely chopped

4 garlic cloves, peeled and crushed

2 tbsp finely chopped fresh root ginger

½ tsp Chinese five-spice powder

100ml (3½fl oz) white wine vinegar

100ml (3½fl oz) lime juice

200g (7oz) thick-cut marmalade

2 large carrots, peeled and cut into 5mm (¼in) cubes

salt and freshly ground black pepper

Yes, it sounds odd, but it really does work. The secret is to get the balance between the chicken being cooked and not overcooked and dry, and the coating sauce nice and sticky. My kids will not eat marmalade, but they will eat this chicken every time.

1 Preheat the oven to 220°C/425°F/Gas 7.

2 Heat half the vegetable oil in a large pan, add the chicken pieces and brown well all over. Remove the chicken from the pan.

3 Add the rest of the oil to the pan, along with the onion, garlic and ginger, and soften slightly for 10 minutes. Add the five-spice, vinegar, lime juice, marmalade and carrots, and stir well. Season well with salt and pepper and cook for 10 minutes, or until syrupy. Take care, it will catch, so stir all the time.

4 Place the chicken into a large shallow ovenproof pan or non-stick baking tray. Carefully pour the sauce over and pop into the preheated oven. Cook for 30 minutes, or until well coloured and cooked through.

5 Remove from the oven and check the chicken is cooked through. Stir well. Leave to rest for 10 minutes, or it will be too hot to eat. The sauce should be nice and thick and coating the chicken well.

6 Serve with baked lime potatoes (see right).

BAKED LIME POTATOES

A simple potato dish that works very well with all roasts. I use a 22cm (8½in) square, 4.5cm (1¾in) deep ceramic baking dish for this amount.

Serves: 4-6

800g (1¾lb) potatoes, peeled
salt and freshly ground black pepper
150ml (5fl oz) strong chicken stock
100ml (3½fl oz) dry white wine
juice of 2 limes
olive oil

1 Preheat the oven to 200°C/400°F/Gas 6.

2 Cut the potatoes in half lengthways, then cut into long wedges, not too thick.

3 Carefully place them in a baking dish, overlapping slightly. Season well with salt and pepper.

4 Boil the chicken stock and wine together in a pan, remove from the stove and stir in the lime juice. Pour over the potatoes, then spoon over 4 tbsp of the olive oil, making sure you coat the cut potatoes.

5 Put the tray in the oven; cook for about 30 minutes, then start to baste the potatoes, regularly, for the next 25-30 minutes, until they are nicely browned and have soaked up the chicken stock, lime juice and wine.

6 Brush the tops with olive oil and serve piled in a bowl.

SEVILLE ORANGE MARMALADE SAUCE

This is a very unusual recipe but it does work well, especially with fattier cuts of meat. Marmalade is not often seen beyond the breakfast menu or dodgy bread and butter puddings, but it can be used in all sorts of ways, provided you understand its complex flavours and make-up. Most barbecue sauces, for instance, are a combination of sweet and sour ingredients and spices. This sauce is no different, and has the added bonus of a sweet and bitter/sour ingredient built in already. Try it, it works very well.

Serves: 6

25ml (1fl oz) vegetable oil
1 small onion, peeled and very finely chopped
20g (¾oz) jarred lemongrass purée
½ level tsp dried red chilli flakes
2 garlic cloves, peeled and crushed
225g (8oz) coarse-chopped marmalade, whizzed to a purée
125ml (4fl oz) cider vinegar
30g (1¼oz) nam pla (Thai fish sauce)
100ml (3½fl oz) water
6 tbsp chopped coriander leaves

1 Heat the oil in a pan, and add the onion, lemongrass purée, dried chilli and garlic, and cook to soften slightly, about 15 minutes.

2 Add the marmalade, vinegar, fish sauce and water. Bring to the boil, stirring well, then reduce the heat to a simmer. You need to reduce the sauce by about half roughly, so it's slightly sticky and gloopy. Take care as the sauce will catch when reducing, due the amount of sugar in the marmalade. Once cooked, remove from the pan, cover and cool.

3 I like to serve this sauce with grilled, braised or barbecued fattier cuts of meat or game.

Jellies or pastilles were all the rage when I was training. They seem to have come back into fashion again now. These days vegetable flavours and textures are also quite common.
I think you need a strong flavour to make a jelly or pastille: blackcurrant, lemon, lime, damson and rhubarb are all great. The secret is to combine sweetness with acidity, and also to attain a nice soft, but chewy texture. Try these, they're very easy.

MARMALADE JELLY PASTILLES

Makes: 300g (10½oz), about 18 jellies

1 x 454g (1lb) jar thick-cut orange marmalade

2 tsp lemon juice

2 tbsp glucose syrup

1-2 pinches citric acid (optional)

3½ tbsp liquid pectin extract

granulated sugar, for dusting

1 Line an 18cm (7in) square tin with baking paper.

2 Liquidize the marmalade to a thick purée.

3 Put the marmalade into a medium non-stick pan with the lemon juice, glucose, citric acid (if using) and pectin. Gently heat the mixture, stirring all the time. Bring to a full boil and boil rapidly for 10 minutes, stirring frequently. The mixture will reduce by about half, and thicken.

4 Remove from the heat, spread into the prepared tin and, when cool, put the tray in the freezer until set to a thick jelly.

5 Leave the tray out of the freezer for a few minutes so that the jelly becomes pliable. Peel the jelly sheet slowly from the paper and fold in half, to double thickness. Slice into strips and then cut into 24 x 2.5cm (1in) lozenges. Sugar your hands if they get sticky.

6 Roll each pastille in granulated sugar, and store in an airtight container in the fridge.

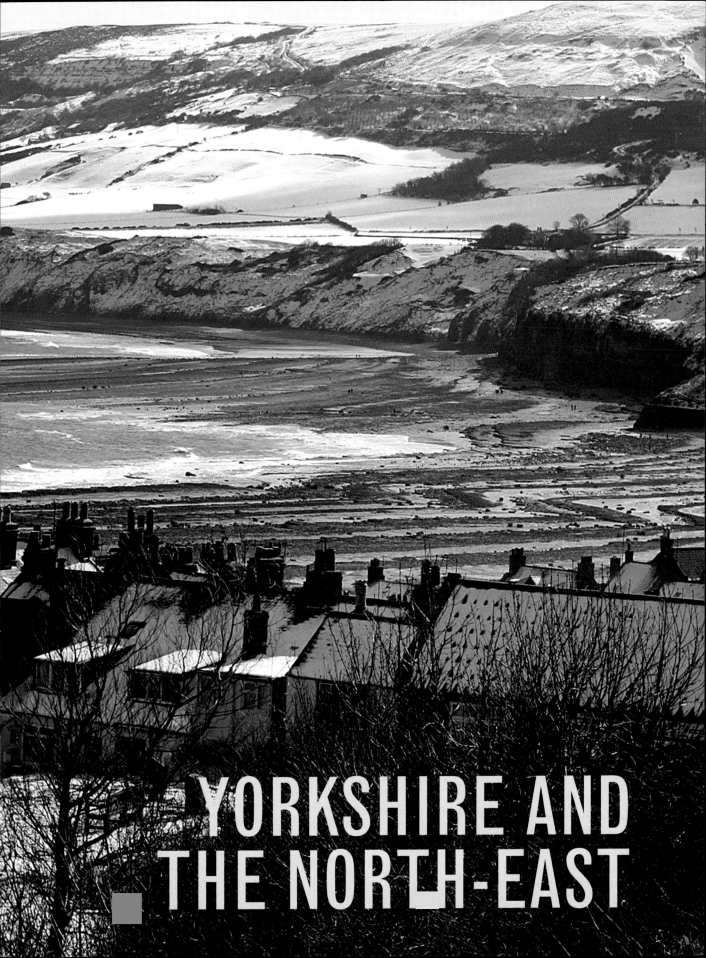

YORKSHIRE AND
THE NORTH-EAST

RHUBARB
E. OLDROYD & SONS

Rhubarb and its myth-laden growing process has always been part of my life. My father was a master at producing the stuff. He used to grow the main-crop variety in large amounts, so at home after dinner we were seldom without large bowls of cold stewed rhubarb and custard. At the time I took it for granted, little realizing exactly what goes into the only UK-grown splash of colour on the greengrocer's stand in January.

It took a visit to West Yorkshire, to see so-called forced rhubarb, to truly appreciate the skill and tender care involved in hand-growing this amazing vegetable (and it is a vegetable, not a fruit).

Leading producer Janet Oldroyd-Hulme is based near the Wakefield point of the famous rhubarb-producing 'triangle' formed by the other two Yorkshire cities of Leeds and Bradford. It was a combination of industrial and geographical suitability that saw this area becoming the UK centre of rhubarb production back in Victorian times. There was plenty of cheap coal to heat the growing sheds, suitable soil, sooty fallout from industry to help fertilize the root-growing fields, good train links, plus a frosty nip from the Pennines that wakens the dormant roots in the depths of winter.

The Oldroyd-Hulmes have been growing forced rhubarb for years, and really know their stuff. 'Forced' rhubarb simply means growing it in the dark to give it an extra succulent flavour, and this can easily be reproduced in your garden by using a large flowerpot to cover the root as it shoots. Going into the heated forcing sheds for the first time is a really eerie experience. When they say 'dark' they mean 'pitch-black'. The workers take great pains to close the main door behind them on entry to keep daylight out, and all the picking of the forced stems is done entirely by candlelight to preserve the soft shoots from bolting. This is also to keep the poisonous but decorative leaves tight, yellow and diamond shaped.

As many as 20,000 crowns are packed into each shed every winter. It was amazing to me how resilient these roots are. They are just plonked down on to a bare earth floor, not even planted, yet they still suck up nutrients. They have so much contained energy they will put out shoots for the next few months until you have beautiful, pink blanched stems. Then each stick is torn from its root by hand. Cutting with a knife can introduce germs to the roots, Janet told me. The forcing season usually starts in late December or sometimes earlier, then runs through until early March, depending on the weather of course.

When I went into the sheds for the first time, my amazement on entry was entirely unforced, if you'll pardon the pun. What a spectacle! I was faced with a forest of spooky knee-high growth, all lit by candles. Spookiest of all, you could hear the rhubarb's 'lust for life'. As we talked, the new shoots were forcing themselves out of the rootballs with a 'popping' sound – it's not often you actually hear something growing.

The forcing sheds are the culmination of a long growing process which starts two to three years earlier when the 'crowns' or rhubarb roots are planted out in the fields and left to grow and store energy. They are then lifted, all loose soil removed and are packed into forcing sheds from late autumn onwards.

You can see all this for yourself by giving them a call. The rhubarb tours in West Yorkshire are very interesting, with great tea and cake afterwards, so book yourself on a visit if you are in the area.

17th February - a very, very cold day in the forced rhubarb season. The rhubarb, grown in the pitch black, is picked in soft candlelight

RHUBARB KETCHUP

Rhubarb makes a great ketchup, and its lovely colour and fine taste make it a real treat in the winter. Ketchups can be made with all sorts of fruits and vegetables and will keep well if sterilized and chilled. Ketchups, or 'catsups' as they were known in the Middle Ages, were originally used to preserve certain fruits and vegetables in liquid form, and included mushroom and onion. The recipe hasn't really changed that much: vinegar, sugar and fruit, just in larger quantities. This ketchup is great with grilled wood-pigeon breast, griddled scallops and boiled or poached white meats such as chicken.

Makes: about 300ml (10fl oz)

500g (18oz) forced rhubarb, cut into 2cm (¾in) chunks, washed well

50ml (2fl oz) cold water

90g (3¼oz) caster sugar

1 large pinch salt

125ml (4fl oz) red wine vinegar

1 tbsp arrowroot

4 tbsp cold water

1 Place the rhubarb in a stainless-steel pan. Add the water and cook over a gentle heat until you have a thick stew, about 10 minutes. Liquidize, then pass through a fine sieve.

2 Add the caster sugar, salt and vinegar to the rhubarb, and bring to the boil.

3 Cook down gently until the sauce is thick, similar to double cream, which will take about 20-25 minutes.

4 Straightaway, pour the ketchup into a sterilized jam jar or Kilner jar. Securely seal and place the jar into a saucepan with a tea-towel or cloth in the base to keep the glass off the bottom of the pan. Pour in enough warm water so that the jar is just covered.

5 Pop a thermometer in the pan and heat the water in the pan to 90°C/194°F (I use a sugar thermometer for this), then turn down the heat and leave for 20 minutes bang on, making sure the temperature stays exactly the same. This will sterilize the ketchup.

6 Carefully remove the hot jar from the water and place on a wooden board or tea-towel, as sometimes the jars will crack if placed on metal or cold surfaces.

7 Cool, then leave for at least a month to mature in a cool dark place (and for up to about 3 months). Once opened eat within a week.

ROAST DUCK WITH RHUBARB STUFFING AND GLAZE

Serves: 4

1 x 1.8kg (4lb) duck

Stuffing

2 tbsp vegetable oil

2 large onions, peeled and finely chopped

2 garlic cloves, peeled and crushed

2 tbsp chopped sage

400g (14oz) good-quality sausagemeat

175ml (6fl oz) cold water

4 tbsp caster sugar

175g (6oz) Oldroyd's rhubarb, forced or main-crop, cut into 1cm (½in) pieces, washed well

1 medium egg

approx. 75-90g (2¾-3¼oz) dried breadcrumbs

salt and freshly ground black pepper

I like my roasting duck to be relatively large, so it's best to buy a duck rather than a duckling, but do take care when buying duck, as they do put on a lot of fat as they get older. Certain breeds, such as the cross-bred Gressingham and the French Barbary, make good roasting birds, but with the added bonus of less fat.

1 Preheat the oven to 200°C/400°F/Gas 6. Prick the bird all over with a fork, just through the skin, not the meat (which would tend to dry it out) and remove any giblets or excess fat.

2 Heat the oil in a saucepan, add the onion, garlic and sage and cook for about 2-3 minutes to soften. Add the sausagemeat and cook for a further 2 minutes to break down. Tip the mixture into a strainer or colander and leave to drain for about 10 minutes.

3 Heat the water, and add the sugar. Once simmering add the rhubarb, and bring back to the boil. Remove from the heat, cover with clingfilm, and leave to cool. Drain well, reserving the syrup.

4 Add the drained rhubarb to the sausagemeat mixture, along with the egg, breadcrumbs and a good dash of salt and pepper. Mix well, but carefully, as you don't want to break up the rhubarb. The stuffing will 'tighten up' once the dried crumbs start to absorb the juices and fat.

5 Fill the bird with the stuffing, and secure the legs with a piece of string. Season the bird all over and rub into the skin. Scrunch a length of foil in the roasting tray to form a sort of pillow. Pop the duck on top so it stays out of the fat.

6 Roast for about 1 hour 25 minutes, or until the juices run clear from an incision in the thigh.

7 Remove the bird from the oven and paint on the reserved syrup from the rhubarb poaching with a pastry brush. Return the duck to the oven increase the heat to 220°C/425°F/Gas 7. Cook until the skin turns crispy, about a further 15 minutes, then repeat the glazing and roasting process. When the bird is completely cooked, remove from the oven and leave to rest for at least 20 minutes before carving.

8 Spoon out the stuffing, then cut the bird into four pieces by removing the legs and cutting the breast in half.

There are many varieties of early rhubarb: Timperley Early, Prince Albert, Fenton Special, Victoria, Reeds Early and my favourite, Stockbridge Arrow, with arrow-shaped leaves. All are excellent for light cooking such as poaching with a little white wine or vermouth, making a delicate sorbet or jelly or mixing with custard to make a fool. Main-crop rhubarb is greener and larger because it is grown outside, and it is eaten later on in the year; this lends itself better to tougher cooking, such as pies, crumbles, jams and pickles. Sweet pickling gives rhubarb a great sweet and sour edge, allowing it to be combined with all sorts of different foods and ingredients. It's perfect with roast duck legs, but also pork and some game (venison and wild duck particularly). It also works well with some fish, such as seared scallops and grilled mackerel, salmon and herring. Rhubarb's acidity balances well with the oily fish. It's also good with strong cheeses such as Stilton, unpasteurized Cheddar and goat's cheese.

SWEET AND SOUR RHUBARB WITH SLOW-ROAST DUCK LEGS

Serves: 4

4 large duck legs, trimmed, knuckle removed

salt and freshly ground black pepper

Sweet and sour rhubarb

150g (5½oz) granulated sugar

100ml (3½fl oz) cold water

1 small onion, peeled and finely chopped

15g (½oz) fresh root ginger, finely chopped

25g (1oz) black peppercorns

8 juniper berries, crushed

approx. 2 tsp sea salt

300g (10½oz) forced rhubarb, cut into 2cm (¾in) pieces, washed well

1 Place all the rhubarb ingredients, apart from the rhubarb, into a stainless-steel saucepan and bring to the boil. Simmer for about 5 minutes. Add the rhubarb and bring back to the boil. Once simmering, take off the stove, cover and leave to cool. Spoon into sterilized Kilner jars and leave in a cool place before serving (or store in a dark place for up to three months).

2 Preheat the oven to 180°C/350°F/Gas 4.

3 Rub the duck legs with salt and pepper, then place on to a non-stick baking tray. Pop into the oven and cook for 50-60 minutes, basting with their own fat occasionally.

4 Once cooked, serve with the sweet preserved rhubarb.

This is such a simple recipe and it is great on ice-cream, pies, trifles, flans, tarts or puddings. The use of champagne is not really necessary; you could use just a dry-medium white wine. But champagne adds a certain decadence to the sauce and, coupled with the fact that you are adding it to one of the best ingredients these shores has to offer, it's well worth the effort and expense. I buy a lot of pink rhubarb in season, and freeze it down for use later in the year. It freezes perfectly and is a welcome treat in the summer. Lightly poached or stewed rhubarb works well in trifles and pavlovas, and makes a perfect companion to English strawberries in an Eton mess.

PINK RHUBARB, STEM GINGER AND CHAMPAGNE ICE-CREAM SAUCE

Serves: 4

500g (18oz) forced rhubarb, cut roughly into 3cm (1¼in) pieces, washed well

55g (2oz) stem ginger in syrup, roughly chopped

55g (2oz) minced lemongrass in oil (from a jar)

125g (4½oz) caster sugar

175ml (6fl oz) Champagne or dry-medium white wine

1 tbsp arrowroot

4 tbsp water

1 Place the rhubarb, ginger, lemongrass, sugar and champagne or wine into a saucepan. Bring to the boil, then cover and simmer for 5 minutes, or until the rhubarb has broken up nicely.

2 Slake the arrowroot with the water, and mix well into the simmering sauce until it thickens nicely. You don't have to thicken the sauce, but I find it holds better once chilled.

3 Liquidize well for a couple of minutes on high speed, then pass through a sieve. Pour into sterilized jars whilst hot, then cool and store in the fridge until needed (it will keep for about 3 weeks).

4 I sometimes preserve the sauce for later in the year. To do that, preserve as for the sweet-and-sour rhubarb chutney on page 211. Cool, then put in the fridge. It will keep for up to 3 months but, once opened, should be eaten within a week.

RHUBARB PASTRY

One thing I love about the French pastry shops are their stunning flans and tarts, they always look so good. This recipe is for a simple fruit pastry using the best ingredients, similar to the ones I have drooled at in pastry shops over the years.

Serves: 4

1 x 375g (13oz) sheet ready-rolled,
all-butter puff pastry

1 large egg yolk

a pinch of salt

Topping

500g (18oz) forced rhubarb,
cut into 3cm (1¼in) pieces

150g (5½oz) caster sugar

juice of ½ lemon

15g (½oz) unsalted butter

2 tsp arrowroot or cornflour

8 fresh lemon balm or mint leaves,
chopped

1 Place the rhubarb, sugar and lemon juice into a stainless-steel saucepan, and cook until soft and pulpy. Then strain well, keeping the juices.

2 Trim the sheet of pastry into a round, roughly 23-24cm (9-9 ½in) across (this is to the width of the sheet of pastry). You can use a dinner plate to cut round. Lay the pastry on a baking sheet, then carefully, using a sharp knife, cut an incision about three-quarters through the pastry, about 1cm (½in) in from the edge all round. It's best to have the pastry as cold as possible when carrying out this task. Then prick the inside of the pastry well with a fork, and put to chill again.

3 Preheat the oven to 200°C/400°F/Gas 6.

4 Mix the egg yolk and salt together well and glaze the edge of the pastry, taking care not to fill in the incision or run over the edge too much (which would stop the pastry rising evenly).

5 Once the rhubarb is strained, spread evenly on to the pastry base, keeping away from the incision. Bake for about 20-25 minutes. The pastry will glaze well and the outside will rise and hold in the rhubarb.

6 Strain the rhubarb syrup into a saucepan and add the butter, then bring to the boil. Once the butter has melted, thicken the sauce with the arrowroot or cornflour, slaked first in a little cold water. The sauce needs to be fairly thick, but you may need to add a little more water if too thick. Finally, add the chopped lemon balm or mint.

7 When the pastry is cooked, remove from the oven and immediately spoon over the warm glaze, including the pastry edges. Leave the whole thing to cool completely.

8 Cut into four slices, and serve with a large blob of clotted cream and a large cappuccino as a morning snack or as part of an afternoon tea.

SCOTLAND

SMOKED SALMON
INVERAWE SMOKED FISH

Thinking back on it, I suppose it was the catalogue that first drew me towards the artisan fish-smokers of Inverawe. Looking beyond the 'By Royal Appointment' crest on the cover, it was the contents that were the real crown-jewels: home-made taramasalata, caviar, smoked eel and, of course, beautifully plump-looking smoked trout and salmon. I was in the car, heading north, at the first opportunity.

Inverawe has been in business since 1974, initially as a fish farm. Up until then, fish-smoking was a cottage, or more accurately a croft, industry, but Robert and Rosie Campbell-Preston of Inverawe spotted a gap in the market for smoked salmon and trout on a commercial scale. The raw materials were plentiful in their neck of the woods, just inland from Oban. I can say this with certainty because during my visit I was taken fly-fishing by Willie, the Inverawe ghillie, and actually saw salmon swim past me. Alas, that was the closest I actually got to catching a wild salmon.

Surrounded by silent and still glens, Inverawe House is an old Campbell clan fortress dating back more than three centuries, a stone's throw from the banks of the River Awe. From small 'back-yard' beginnings as Scotland's first commercial smokehouse, Inverawe has gone from strength to strength. It now has nine brick kilns all puffing away round the clock to meet demand.

On my visit, I met up with Lucy Thornhill, one of the few female smokers in the business, still only in her twenties but with an experienced head on young shoulders. She told me each kiln has the potential to smoke 100 fish at a time. The smoke comes from locally supplied oak logs, which are placed in braziers in the kilns, and need replenishing up to five times a day to do the job properly. Whereas a commercial smoker would use wood-chips, pressurised to blast out enough oak smoke to cure a side of fish in six hours or so, at Inverawe it takes as long as it takes. Lucy explained to me that their kilns take two days or more to smoke the fish properly. Like a chimney, some of the kilns 'draw' better than others and the process is even affected by the weather and seasons. From experience Lucy has established that nice crisp autumn days provide the best conditions for smoking fish. Up here in the Highlands, they say, 'A good clothes-drying day is a good fish-smoking day'.

As with so many things, the quality of the raw material is crucial to the finished item. Inverawe source organic fish from the Shetlands as well as local, carefully farmed salmon, which get plenty of freedom in cages sited in fast-flowing waters. These fish are noticeably less flabby than the 'normal' farmed salmon, and make for a beautifully dense end-product. I was amazed just how pale this 'real' smoked salmon is. And as well as 'cold-smoking', where the salmon hangs above gently percolating oak smoke, Inverawe also produces salmon, eel and trout that have been 'hot-smoked' over a much fiercer charcoal brazier, which cooks the fish at the same time.

The more I saw of this artisan fish-smoking operation, the more impressed I became. Even before the salmon and trout are smoked, they must be cured by layering them in salt to remove excess water. The thickness of the salt crust is dictated by the density of the fillet to be smoked, and of course years of experience by the dedicated team.

I could hardly leave Inverawe without enjoying the fat of the land – and sea – so I was invited to a feast of smoked eel, trout, mackerel, haddock and even wild halibut, not forgetting a side order of Scottish Highland caviar. A meal fit for Bonnie Prince Charlie.

W F

SMOKED SALMON AND PICKLED BEETROOT WITH SOFT-BOILED EGGS AND CELERY SALT

Serves: 4

12 pickled baby beetroots, halved and rinsed well

600g (1lb 5oz) sliced smoked salmon, cut roughly into 2cm (¾in) strips

6 tbsp extra virgin olive oil

1 tsp cracked black pepper

a pinch of salt

4 soft-boiled eggs (4 minutes), carefully peeled

4 tbsp celery salt

I have no problem using jarred pickled beetroots, in fact I adore them. You can pickle your own, like my Dad and my wife do, but to be honest they taste almost the same once doused in vinegar for three months. The sweet, sharp flavour complements many foods such as terrines, cooked cold meats, and all cheeses, and it's even great with eggs and bacon at breakfast time. It also works well with smoked fish; a little does go a long way. Here combined with the oiliness and smoky flavour of the salmon, coupled with warm egg yolks and sprinkled with celery salt, it's a match made in heaven.

1 Once rinsed and drained, pat the beetroots with a piece of kitchen paper, then place in a large bowl. Add the smoked salmon, olive oil, cracked pepper and salt, and mix carefully.

2 Top with the soft-boiled eggs, unbroken if possible. Sprinkle with plenty of celery salt.

3 Once at the table, crack the eggs and let people help themselves, it's as simple as that. Serve with crusty bread.

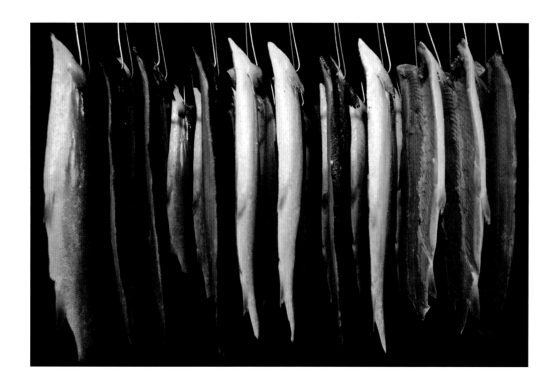

December- Hundreds of salmon were filleted,
salted and smoked for the Christmas rush
on this cold, cold day

ASPARAGUS AND SMOKED SALMON WITH PEA AND TARRAGON CRÈME FRAÎCHE

Serves: 6

1kg (2¼lb) young English asparagus

salt and freshly ground black pepper

600g (1lb 5oz) smoked salmon, sliced

Crème fraîche

500g (18oz) crème fraîche

2 tbsp roughly chopped tarragon

2 tbsp cider vinegar

2 tsp caster sugar

250g (9oz) baby frozen peas, cooked, refreshed and drained

Sometimes you come across great combinations: chocolate and pear, coffee and walnut, ice-cream and raspberry sauce, chicken and lobster. This is one of those. Nothing can be better than English asparagus, perfectly cooked, and great Scottish smoked salmon. It's just perfect. All you can do is add something to help them on their way. Frozen baby peas are an absolute joy, and work well with salmon and asparagus. I love them added to crème fraîche or mayonnaise, sharpened with a little cider vinegar, and the addition of tarragon really works well.

1 Trim the ends of the asparagus, so you don't end up with woody stems.

2 Bring a large pan of salted boiling water to a rapid boil. Plunge the asparagus into the boiling water, bring back to the boil, then boil for 1 minute. Immediately lift the asparagus out with a slotted spoon and plunge into iced water. This arrests the cooking, and keeps the brilliant green colour in the tender stems. Once cooked, drain well and chill well.

3 Meanwhile, mix the crème fraiche with the tarragon, some salt and pepper, the cider vinegar, sugar and well-drained peas.

4 To finish, wrap each slice of smoked salmon around five or six stems of asparagus.

5 Pile on to a serving plate, then pile the pea crème fraîche next to the asparagus rolls. Serve with crusty bread, a little extra olive oil and plenty of black pepper.

SIMPLE SMOKED SALMON KEDGEREE

Serves: 2

100g (3½oz) unsalted butter

5 spring onions, roughly chopped

100g (3½oz) flat mushrooms, sliced

350g (12oz) cooked long-grain rice

salt and freshly ground black pepper

1-2 pinches curry powder (optional)

250g (9oz) smoked salmon, sliced into thin strips

4 tbsp roughly chopped parsley

2 hard-boiled eggs, shelled and roughly chopped

I love kedgeree made with natural smoked haddock, but smoked salmon also works really well. Traditionally served at breakfast, kedgeree also makes a really nice light lunch or even brunch dish. The secret is the butter, and plenty of it, it really adds to the flavour, and brings all the textures, colours and flavours together. Almost any cooked protein will work in kedgeree, just remember not to overcook the fish.

1 Heat half the butter in a wok, but do not allow to colour. Add the spring onions and cook for 1 minute, then add the mushrooms and cook until limp, about a further minute.

2 Stir in the cooked rice with a good seasoning of salt and pepper and a pinch of curry powder, and warm through.

3 Remove the pan from the heat and stir in the smoked salmon, most of the parsley, the rest of the unsalted butter and the chopped boiled eggs, then stir well. Warm through on top of the stove for a couple of minutes, but do not overcook.

4 Serve straightaway, with a really good sprinkling of parsley.

PASTA WITH SMOKED SALMON,

Serves: 4

175g (6oz) baby broad beans

3 tbsp olive oil

3 spring onions, sliced on the diagonal

2 tbsp chopped coriander leaves

500g (18oz) dried rigatoni pasta, cooked and drained

10 black olives, stoned and quartered

225g (8oz) smoked salmon, cut into thin strips

salt and freshly ground black pepper

1 tbsp lemon juice

To serve

soured cream

chopped fresh chives

Broad beans are delicious, and are extremely good value for money. Most chefs would never use frozen broad beans, but they will use frozen peas. What's the difference? They are both superb. That aside, broad beans are a perfect accompaniment to smoked salmon.

I know smoked salmon is expensive, but, because it has such a distinct, strong flavour, a little goes a long way. And if you buy the trimmings or end cuts, a little can go a very long way. The secret here is to not overcook the salmon, just make sure it is warm and not too hot.

1 Add the frozen beans to a pan of boiling water, bring back to the boil and then simmer for about 2 minutes. Strain well and keep warm.

2 Heat the olive oil in a wok (don't let it get too hot) then add the spring onions and cook for a few seconds to soften. Add the coriander and cooked pasta then season well and cook for about 3 minutes to heat through. Do not overcook.

3 Add the warm broad beans and black olives to the pasta with the smoked salmon and toss to combine then cook for about 1-2 minutes to warm through. Be careful you don't overcook the salmon, it must remain opaque. Season well, and add a squeeze of lemon juice.

4 Serve in a deep bowl, topped with a spoonful of soured cream and plenty of chopped chives.

BEEF
YOUR LOCAL BUTCHER

When I go shopping for beef, indeed all meats for that matter, I want to know a few basic facts about what I'm buying:

• Has the beast been reared and kept well?
• Has the beast been fed correctly?
• Has the beast been slaughtered humanely?
• Has the meat been hung correctly, and butchered and stored properly?

Chances are, if these criteria have been adhered to, you will end up with a delicious steak or Sunday roast. I generally seek out, cook and eat Aberdeen Angus, but have recently cooked, eaten and enjoyed Longhorn and Dexter.

It seems that not a day goes by without reading of some 'must-buy' new breed. Whilst this is obviously a good thing (and I applaud all beef producers for their determination and true grit in the face of appalling set-backs in recent years), the chances are that most of these fabled strains of beef cattle will only be seen and eaten by a lucky few. Most rare beef cuts come from bespoke 'cottage' producers, selling locally through farm-shops, or by mail-order.

Besides choice for the consumer, price is also important. Almost three-quarters of all beef reared and consumed in Britain is sold through the supermarkets. Shoppers get used to buying indifferent cuts of beef and other meats at supermarket prices and even find those dear. They baulk at paying extra for a specific breed or small producer, even if it tastes noticeably better. I actually asked my wife not to buy meat at a certain supermarket because I could not believe its poor quality. It was too red, weeping blood, sweating and flaccid in its obligatory clingfilm-wrapped polystyrene tray. Cooked, the meat was tough, tasteless and frankly awful.

One of the problems is that the longer you hang a carcass, the more moisture – and hence weight – is lost; consequently, the less profit you make. It all comes down to money with the big suppliers.

Personally, I like my beef to be hung for a minimum of 21 days and up to 28 days. After that, if it is not looked after with great skill and experience, I find the meat can take on a rancid smell and flavour.

On the back of these easily learned lessons, I struck up a relationship with my local butcher, Derek Babb. Of the old school, he sells his own dry-cured bacon and his rump steaks are superb, full of flavour, nice and dry to the touch. We have had many conversations regarding the public's perception of what good meat should look like. I gently rib him, saying 'No way would you see that in a supermarket', looking at a lovely dark, purpley, crusty, three-week-aged forerib on the bone. He agrees.

Derek's meat in his chiller cabinet looks dark and almost rimed to the eye. His bacon is dull in colour with none of the pinkness of supermarket pork. His chickens look nice, dry and ready to roast. Tripe, lambs' hearts, oxtail and Barnsley lamb chops, all sell well, so 'Why?', I ask him. He replies, 'All my customers know what I sell, and they like it.' And indeed one thing I have noticed whilst in Derek's shop is that his clientele are all of a certain age, to put it delicately. Generations older than mine have learned well, have a butcher's eye for good meat, and invariably know how to cook it.

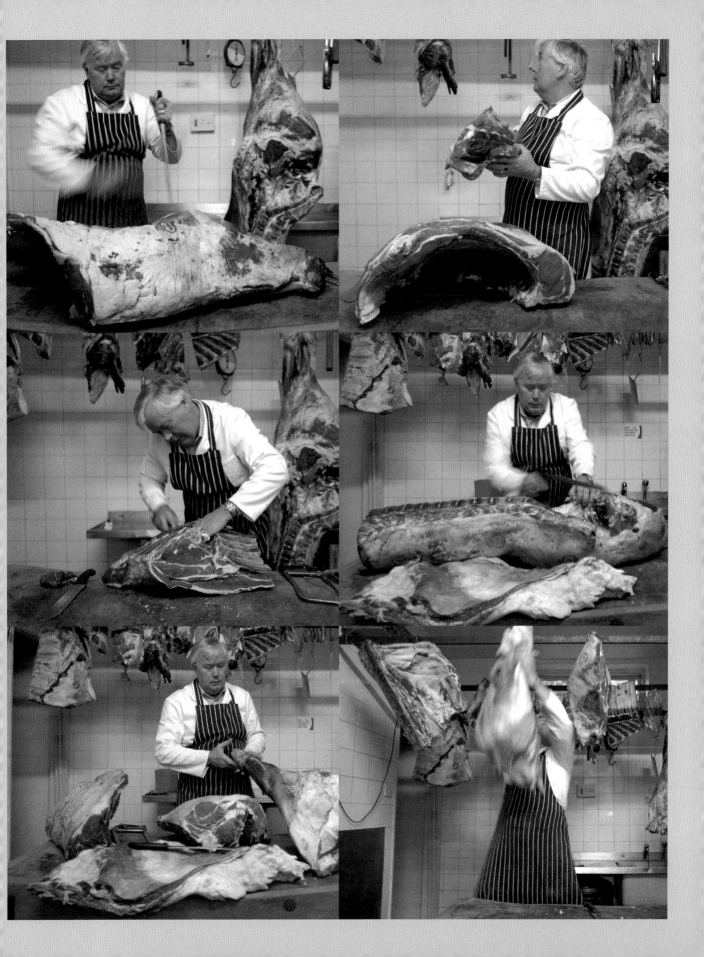

One of the nicest raw dishes is beef tartare. Basically, it's a mixture of chopped raw, fresh-as-can-be fillet of beef, capers, gherkins, shallots, oil and a little vinegar, which are seasoned and brought together with a raw egg yolk. It's traditionally mixed in front of you at the table and served with thin, crisp allumettes (chips). To most people it's an absolute no-no, but it can be very good. The problem that can occur, and I emphasize the word 'can', is cross-contamination: the transfer of bacteria from raw and cooked foods, or infection from raw egg yolks. Having said that, I have eaten beef tartare many times and I have never had a problem. The only thing I would say is use scrupulously fresh ingredients, and take basic hygiene precautions.

Serves: 4

400g (14oz) aged beef fillet, roughly cut into 8 x 55g (2oz) pieces

1 large bunch of British watercress

extra virgin olive oil

Sauce

5 tbsp good-quality creamed horseradish sauce

5 tsp wholegrain mustard

2 pinches chilli powder

a pinch of caster sugar

2 tbsp finely chopped tarragon

4 tbsp vegetable oil

2 tbsp extra virgin olive oil

a little water

MARINATED BEEF WITH HORSERADISH, CHILLI AND WATERCRESS

1 Beat the fillet pieces out between two pieces of lightly wetted plastic, as thin as possible, and then chill well.

2 Make up the sauce by adding all the ingredients to a bowl apart from the oils and water. Gradually add both oils, until the sauce is thick and creamy. Finally add a little water, until you have a sauce that is thick enough to coat the beef fillet, but not so thin that it will run off. It should be the thickness of double cream.

3 To serve, carefully coat each of the raw thin slices of beef in the sauce, on both sides. Then arrange flat on a large plate, slightly overlapping. Top with a large handful of watercress, lightly dressed with extra virgin olive oil.

PEPPERPOT BEEF AND ORANGE STEW

Serves: 4

500g (18oz) braising steak, diced

2 tbsp vegetable oil

2 tbsp plain flour

1 tbsp tomato purée

1 small red onion, peeled and chopped

1 red and 1 yellow pepper, seeded and chopped

25g (1oz) fresh root ginger, grated

1 small red chilli, seeded and chopped

1 x 410g (14¼oz) can kidney beans, drained and well rinsed

1 small orange, cut into 6 wedges

1 beef stock cube, crumbled

2 tbsp roughly chopped coriander leaves

salt and freshly ground black pepper

To serve (optional)

soured cream

chopped fresh parsley

Autumn is a great time to enjoy a hearty stew. Here's one with a twist, the oranges and ginger giving it a really different slant. Serve it with soured cream poured over the top and lots of chopped parsley.

1 Preheat the oven to 180°C/350°F/Gas 4.

2 Using kitchen paper, pat the meat dry. Heat 1 tbsp of the oil in a deep casserole dish or ovenproof pan, then add the meat and cook until browned all over, about 10 minutes. Sprinkle on the flour and stir in well with the tomato purée.

3 Heat the remaining oil in a frying pan. Add the onion, peppers, ginger and chilli, and cook gently until softened and golden brown, about 10 minutes. Tip the mixture into the casserole dish with the beef and stir together.

4 Place half the kidney beans in a food processor with enough cold water to just cover, blitz until smooth, then stir into the beef mixture. Add the orange wedges, remaining beans, stock cube and coriander and some salt and pepper.

5 Bring to the boil on top of the stove, then cover the dish with a tight-fitting lid. Cook for about 2 hours or until the beef is tender.

6 Serve straight from the pot with, if you like, a spoonful of soured cream and some chopped parsley on top.

TWICE-COOKED BEEF SHORT RIBS

Serves: 4

4 short beef ribs, about 1.3kg (3lb) in weight

2 medium onions, peeled and roughly chopped

1 medium carrot, peeled and roughly chopped

2 garlic cloves, peeled and chopped

1 small sprig each of thyme and rosemary

3 beef stock cubes

Rub

1½ tbsp English mustard powder

10-15 juniper berries, crushed

3 tbsp garlic powder or granules

1 tsp cracked black pepper

1 tsp dried thyme

Mop sauce

2 tbsp runny honey

1 tbsp Worcestershire sauce

2 tbsp malt vinegar

2 tbsp creamed horseradish

1 tbsp extra virgin olive oil

The basis for this recipe I picked up in North Carolina, when I was researching real smoking and barbecuing, involving long, slow, temperature-controlled cooking. It was probably one of the best things I have ever done. The thought and careful planning that goes into real barbecued and smoked food is amazing. Buy the well-hung ribs with plenty of meat and fat on. The same process can be applied to spare ribs (belly) and breast of lamb ribs.

1 Place the ribs, onion, carrot, garlic, thyme, rosemary and stock cubes into a large saucepan. Cover with cold water and bring to the boil. Skim well and reduce the heat to a very gentle simmer. This is really important: if the meat cooks too quickly, it becomes stringy, tough and dry. Cook, mostly covered, very slowly for about 2½ hours. Once cooked, the meat will be very soft, but *not* falling off the bone. Cool and then chill in the stock.

2 The next day remove the chilled fat from the stock and take out the ribs. Dry well with kitchen paper. (Freeze the stock for other dishes.)

3 Make up the rub mix by crushing very well, or placed in a spice grinder until you have a fine mix or rub. Sprinkle over the ribs, pressing down, making sure they are covered well. Cover and leave to marinate for at least an hour, best overnight if possible.

4 Heat a grill or barbecue until the grill is nearly full heat or the coals are grey. Too hot in both cases and the ribs will burn before they have warmed through. A good technique for the barbecue is when you can place your hand roughly 4cm (1½in) above the coals and say '1001, 1002, 1003, 1004' without taking your hand away.

5 Mix the mop sauce ingredients together well.

6 Carefully place the ribs on the hot grill and cook for 15-18 minutes, turning occasionally. Brush or spoon the mop sauce over the ribs every few minutes. This will give them a beautiful flavour and colour. Take care, as the ribs will burn if they get too hot.

7 Remove the ribs from the grill and eat hot with a little extra English mustard or creamed horseradish liberally smeared over. I serve mine on their own.

SALT-CRUST ROAST FORERIB OF BEEF

For some reason chefs seem to only use sirloin of beef for their Sunday roast, saying that it's the best cut. I think there are other great roasting joints that eat equally well as, if not better than, sirloin. Provided you do your research on not only the cut, but also on how long the meat has been hung, the end-result can be spectacular. Two other determining factors are the temperature you cook at, and length of time you cook the meat for. Rump and topside are two classic examples. Not being hung for long enough, and cooking too quickly, will ruin these two cuts.

There is a lot to be said about the length of time meat is hung for. Certainly it makes a huge difference to the eating quality. For beef, I reckon a minimum of 21 days, 28 to 30 even better. After that I think it takes on a slightly tainted, often unpleasant flavour, and to me does not demonstrably tenderize further.

Trimmed forerib is also a cracker, due to its good marbling of fat. And remember, it's the other end of the sirloin, so it will be tender. But what you have to do is cook it in a cooler oven, and for slightly longer, or it will toughen and dry out. This method is the only really successful way of cooking the rib beautifully. Don't worry about the salt content, it makes the end result gorgeous and not at all salty. Cooking this way keeps in the moisture, ensuring the result is spot on, every time.

Serves: 8

1 x 3-rib forerib of beef, about 5kg (roughly 11lb in old money), hung for at least 21 days

4-5 heaped tbsp dry mustard powder

freshly ground black pepper

1.5kg (3lb 5oz) strong white flour

500g (18oz) salt

8 large egg whites

about 600ml (1 pint) cold water

1 Spread the dry mustard powder and plenty of black pepper all over the rib and leave for about 3 hours at room temperature.

2 Preheat the oven to 170°C/325°F/Gas 3.

3 Next, pop the flour, salt and egg whites into a mixing bowl and bring together, then add enough water to form a stiff but pliable dough. Remove from the bowl, form the dough into a blanket and spread over the whole joint, bone and all.

4 Once the joint is completely covered, place in a baking tray, pop into the oven and cook for 2½ hours.

5 Take the rib out of the oven, and remove the by-now hardened salt crust. Throw it away.

6 Turn up the oven to 230°C/450°F/Gas 8. Put the rib back in to glaze and brown. This will take 20-30 minutes, depending on your oven.

7 Remove the meat from the oven, cover with foil, and leave for 20 minutes before carving. The meat will be beautifully pink.

OX TONGUE WITH GHERKINS AND MASH

Before cooking, you must soak the tongue in cold water, changing the water a couple of times, for at least 24 hours.

Serves: 6-8

1 large pickled ox tongue, about 1.5kg (3lb 5oz), soaked for at least 24 hours (see above)

2 carrots, peeled and left whole

2 medium onions, peeled and left whole

2 celery stalks

1 small leek, washed well and left whole

4 tbsp malt vinegar

a few black peppercorns

1kg (2¼lb) potatoes, peeled

140g (5oz) unsalted butter

600ml (1 pint) good gravy or sauce

12 small gherkins, finely sliced

4 tbsp vinegar from the gherkins

2 tbsp double cream

1 Wash the soaked tongue in plenty of cold water. Place in a large saucepan and add the vegetables, vinegar and peppercorns. Cover with water and bring to the boil, then turn down the heat, put the lid on and simmer gently for 3 hours, or until a skewer can pass easily through the thickest part of the meat.

2 Meanwhile boil the potatoes until well cooked, then mash well and add the butter, black pepper and salt and mix well. Keep warm.

3 Heat the gravy, add the gherkins and vinegar, and mix well. Add the cream and stir. Keep warm.

4 Once the tongue is cooked, remove from the cooking liquor. Wearing rubber gloves, carefully peel the skin from the hot tongue with your fingers. To serve, cut the tongue into thick slices and lay on top of the mash. Spoon the sauce over.

CORNED BEEF HASH

Corned beef hash comes in many guises. The basic recipe has not changed for many years, and is still loved all over the world. My Auntie Joey makes the best corned beef hash, and this recipe is based on the one she cooked for us years ago. It needs to be served with a pickle to offset the richness. My Dad's red cabbage is great, and pickled walnuts are good too.

Serves: 2

3 tbsp vegetable oil

1 large onion, peeled and finely chopped

300g (10½oz) potatoes, peeled and roughly cut into 3cm (1¼in) pieces

approx. 400ml (14fl oz) beef stock, boiling

3 tbsp Worcestershire sauce

salt and freshly ground black pepper

250g (9oz) chilled corned beef, cut into 3cm (1¼in) pieces

3 tbsp roughly chopped parsley

1 Heat the vegetable oil in an ovenproof pan. Add the onion and cook over a moderate heat to take a little colour, about 5 minutes, then add the potatoes and stir. Add the beef stock, Worcestershire sauce, salt and pepper and bring back to the boil. Cover, turn the heat down and simmer gently or pop in a moderate oven for 20 minutes, until the potatoes are cooked and starting to break up. The stock is thickened by the potato breaking down, but still leaving some solids. You may need to add a touch more stock.

2 Once the potatoes are ready, add the chunks of corned beef, stir well and heat through for a further 5 minutes. Do not overcook or the beef will fall apart.

3 Add the roughly chopped parsley and season with salt, pepper and a little more Worcestershire sauce. Serve with pickled red cabbage and pickled walnuts.

WHISKY
EDRADOUR

I've been to some factories in my time, but the Edradour distillery near Pitlochry in Scotland is the most unlikely looking manufacturing plant I've ever seen. Comfy in its tree-lined valley, Edradour is a picture-postcard collection of white-painted buildings, the doors and windows picked out in post-office red.

Originally a barley farmers' co-operative, Edradour dates back to 1825, when whisky-making was legalized. Today, unlike many Scottish distilleries, it is still fiercely independent. Edradour produces 90,000 litres of 70 proof 'goldie' a year. It might sound a lot, but it's a mere 12 casks a week. Nevertheless this pint-sized operation suits head distiller Ian Henderson just fine. He's worked in distilleries all over Scotland and was persuaded to defer retirement to turn his considerable skills to running Edradour. He has just two colleagues, Jimmie and Neil.

I felt guilty dragging a third of Edradour's workforce away from the production line, but Ian had everything well under control. When he ushered me into the first building on my tour, the room was billowing clouds of steam as scalding water was poured on to the prepared barley to create the 'wort'.

Unlike some distilleries, where you'll see a long row of stills (the strangely shaped giant copper flasks that heat the liquid into steam), Edradour has only two. One of these has had to have running repairs from a local blacksmith, who apparently took great pains to hammer some dents into his new copper patches to match the original battered metalwork. Distillers have a fear of the new, and it's believed the still's dents and creases contribute to the distinctive flavour of each whisky. Each time the fermented yeast-water-barley based liquid is heated and collected as steam,

then cooled, it gets stronger. Edradour do it twice – 'double-distilling' – and Ian took me round the back to show me the cooling ponds or 'worm-tubs', where coils of iron tubing wind through a small pond. Of course, the Edradour distillery is bisected by a stream so there is never any shortage of water to make whisky with and to cool the process down. These Highland distilleries were not placed where they were by accident.

For whisky to get the legal right to be called 'Scotch', it needs storing in barrels for a minimum of three years. Our last port of call was the whisky store, a highly secure but atmospheric old building. Where once a local cooper would have been on hand to churn out new barrels for the many Scottish distilleries, these days the barrels used for storing and maturing whisky come second-hand from the Spanish sherry industry and the American bourbon businesses. Each gradually infuses its own distinctive residual colour and flavour into the newly made 'white' spirit over the decade or so that Ian likes to store his whiskies for.

Ian's skill lies not only in making the whisky, but in the subsequent blending of different batches, different years and different barrels to produce the recognizably flowery flavour and golden colour of Edradour. The all-important term 'single malt' of course means that Ian doesn't blend his whisky with anyone else's.

That night in one of the country-house hotels the Scots do so well, I met up with Annabel Meikle of the Scotch Malt Whisky Society. I needed to put what I'd seen that day into perspective with a little help from a wee dram or three. Helpfully for this novice, Annabel simplified the whole business by bringing bottles to represent the three characteristic types of Scotch single malt whisky – Lowland, Speyside and Islay.

Three whiskies, and all very different, but what gladdened my heart was that the tiny Edradour distillery product I'd seen being made, and had tasted, can hold its own against virtually any single malt made today, testimony to the three men who work there. I'm glad I made the journey to visit them.

WHISKY JELLY WITH OATMEAL CREAM

Serves: 4

Jelly

150ml (5fl oz) single malt whisky

400ml (14fl oz) cold water

115g (4oz) unrefined caster sugar

3 gelatine leaves, soaked in cold water until soft

juice of ½ lemon

Oatmeal cream

115g (4oz) oats

4 tbsp granulated brown sugar

1 x 264ml (9½fl oz) tub double cream, very lightly whipped

Quite an odd jelly this, but it's an old combination, which is very simple to make and a nice way to end a heavy meal.

1 Pour the whisky, water and sugar into a saucepan and just warm through until the sugar has dissolved.

2 Remove from the heat, add the soaked gelatine leaves, and stir until dissolved. Finally, add the lemon juice and stir well. Pour into four small tumblers or into a large bowl. Cover with clingfilm and chill until set.

3 Preheat the oven to 180°C/350°F/Gas 4.

4 Mix together the oats and sugar and carefully toast in the oven, until nice and crunchy, about 6-8 minutes, then cool. Do not burn.

5 Mix the oats into the cream lightly. Pile on top of the jelly if it's in the large bowl or, if the jelly is in tumblers, top with a nice scoop of the oatmeal cream. Serve with fingers of butter shortbread.

GRILLED SALMON WITH WHISKY AND MIRIN GLAZE

Serves: 4

4 x 140g (5oz) salmon steaks, skin on, but scaled

Glaze

100ml (3½fl oz) water

3 tsp creamed horseradish

100ml (3½fl oz) whisky, preferably single malt

90g (3¼oz) dark brown unrefined sugar

100ml (3½fl oz) mirin

2 tbsp dark soy sauce

2 tsp tamarind paste

salt and cracked black pepper

2 tbsp olive oil

1 tsp grated lemon zest

1 tsp garlic powder

2 tsp arrowroot

a little water

This glaze works very well with most fish or meat that are to be grilled. The reason I starch the glaze is so it will cling to the protein well, and impart a lovely mellow flavour. The combination of whisky and mirin (a type of rice wine) also adds an unusual, but warm, full flavour to the glaze.

1 Place the water, horseradish, whisky, sugar, mirin, soy, tamarind, salt, pepper, oil, lemon zest and garlic powder into a saucepan and bring to the boil. Simmer until the sugar has dissolved. Add enough arrowroot slaked in a little water, to thicken nicely. Do not over-thicken. Cook for 1 minute then remove from the stove, cool and chill well.

2 Preheat the grill to moderately high.

3 Place the salmon steaks skin-side down on a tray. Brush heavily with half the glaze. Reserve the rest for dipping in later.

4 Grill the salmon for 10 minutes, glazing all the time. Do not overcook. The sauce will stick and glaze nicely.

5 Once cooked, remove the salmon from the grill and leave to rest for 5 minutes. Serve on hot plates, with a green salad, a few new potatoes and some glaze for dipping.

BRAMLEY APPLE AND WHISKY COMPOTE

This compote will go with any white meat but particularly with fattier cuts such as belly pork, pork chops and roasted chicken. It's also good with game, whether it's in terrine or potted form, or just plain roasted. I also think it works bizarrely well with pheasant curry. The secret is using a tart apple such as a Bramley or even a Howgate Wonder.

Serves: 4

3 large Bramley apples, peeled, cored and roughly chopped
100ml (3½fl oz) cider vinegar
100g (3½oz) unrefined golden caster sugar
3 tbsp dry white wine
100ml (3½fl oz) whisky, preferably single malt
1 vegetable stock cube
a pinch of ground turmeric
2 pinches ground allspice
salt and freshly ground black pepper
55g (2oz) butter

1 Place the apple, vinegar, sugar, wine and whisky, stock cube, turmeric and allspice into a pan. Place on the stove and bring to the boil. Cover and turn down the heat, then cook slowly until thick and reduced, stirring from time to time, about 15 minutes. You may need to add a little water if the compote becomes too thick and dry.

2 Season with salt and pepper, and then add the butter. Cook until nice and pulpy, but not too smooth, another 10 minutes or so.

3 Serve with grilled or roasted chicken or pork.

CHOC AND NUT COOKIES WITH WHISKY ICING

One of the best things about American food are the soft squidgy cookies they serve with coffee or at breakfast. Having cooked in America, I had to include a recipe, but with a Scottish twist, of course.

Makes: 10 cookies

115g (4oz) unsalted butter, softened
115g (4oz) caster sugar
6 tbsp condensed milk
200g (7oz) self-raising flour
90g (3¼oz) white chocolate, roughly chopped
55g (2oz) roasted salted peanuts, chopped
Icing
140g (5oz) fondant icing sugar, sieved
2 tbsp whisky, preferably single malt
2 tbsp double cream

1 Cream the butter and sugar together for 2-3 minutes until soft and creamy. Mix in the condensed milk, flour, chocolate and peanuts. Form the dough into a large, squat sausage shape, 10cm (4in) long, 8cm (3¼in) wide. Roll in clingfilm and chill well.

2 Preheat the oven to 150°C/300°F/Gas 2. Line two baking trays with baking paper.

3 Remove the clingfilm and cut the sausage into 10 x 5mm (¼in) slices. Space the slices out on the lined baking trays – the cookies will spread during cooking.

4 Bake for about 10-12 minutes until slightly risen and light brown. Do not overcook. Remove from the oven and leave to cool before trying to remove from the baking tray. Cool completely.

5 Make the icing by mixing all the ingredients together. Spread carefully on to the cookies then leave to set.

WHISKY
TEATIME CAKE

Makes: 1 small loaf

175g (6oz) currants

85g (3oz) sultanas

90ml (3fl oz) whisky, preferably
single malt

1 tbsp lemon juice

350g (12oz) plain flour

1 tsp mixed spice

175g (6oz) dark brown raw cane sugar

1½ level tsp bicarbonate of soda

175g (6oz) butter or margarine

150ml (5fl oz) milk

A lot of fruit cakes are either dry or crumbly or both, but not this recipe. It's best to soak the fruit in the whisky and lemon juice overnight; it makes a real difference to the final texture.

1 Soak the dried fruit in the whisky and lemon juice for at least 2 hours, or best overnight.

2 Preheat the oven to 180°C/350°F/Gas 4. Line a 900g (2lb) loaf tin with baking paper.

3 Put the flour, spice, sugar and bicarbonate of soda into a large mixing bowl and rub in the butter or margarine. Mix in the soaked fruit but do not over-work or the cake will end up chewy to eat, as you will strengthen the gluten in the flour. Gradually stir in the milk, to end up with a soft dropping consistency.

4 Spoon the mixture into the tin and bake for about 50 minutes, or until firm to the touch and a skewer inserted comes out clean.

5 Leave to cool on a wire rack and then turn out. Slice and spread thickly with salted butter. Perfect.

IRELAND

HONEY
BEEKEEPING

Before I went to Ireland, I had no idea there was so much to keeping bees and making honey. My guide to all things 'apiaristic' was to be veteran beekeeper Philip McCabe, whom I met north of Dublin.

Philip helped me don the full bee-keeping space-suit before approaching the hives. It is a slightly scary experience to be near hives with the bees buzzing around your gauze mask. As we knelt down in front of the hives, the buzzing reached a crescendo. My instincts were to run away but Philip was a very calming influence, telling me to relax. Bees can tell if you are tense, rather worryingly.

Before dismantling a hive to show me its inner workings, Philip pumped in some smoke to make the bees sleepy. At the mouth of the hive, where the bees land and depart, he pointed out some workers doing a special 'waggle-dance', a carefully choreographed series of movements to show other workers where

good sources of nectar and pollen are. As the day progressed, the more I learnt about these insects, the more impressed I became.

Most hives contain a community of 20,000 bees, but some can reach a hectic 120,000. At this stage they are likely to swarm, which means the bees decide to desert the hive. It takes experience as a beekeeper to spot and prevent this.

Bees are non-stop workers throughout the summer months, quietening down in winter when there's no nectar or pollen about. At this stage, the beekeeper feeds them on sugary water because the chances are he has removed the honey the colony would naturally survive on.

Back indoors, Philip explained to me how honey can vary from hive to hive, year to year, even depending on the time of year, and especially according to which pollen the bees have been collecting. It's amazing how much the colour of honey can vary too. Oil-seed rape, for instance, produces a very crystalline honey, whilst lime trees, common in London, produce a softer, runnier honey. At Philip's insistence I tasted a port-wine coloured honey with a very powerful flavour that came from Irish ling heather.

We stayed at An Grianán, which is a residential college for all sorts of subjects. One of the best-known of An Grianán's tutors is veteran Irish television cook, Marie McGuirk. She cooked up a storm for our benefit, using Philip McCabe's honey. The dishes included honey cheesecake, a wonderful oaty brown bread, muffins, scones, fruit salad, chilli chicken and honey-baked Boyne salmon. Marie runs cookery demonstrations on Irish home cooking and they are always packed out. I can see why.

Our next port of call was to the bees of the nearby Sisters of Mercy convent. There the hives are tended by Sister Catherine, Sister Monica and 90-year-old Sister Paul. Up until a year before we visited, Sister Paul had made all the hives herself, but now she oversees the operation.

The honey is extracted from the racks of honeycomb by centrifugal force. Philip does it by machine but it's still done by hand at the convent. Then the honey is strained and jarred up. Alternatively honey is boxed and sold in perfect 1lb combs, bees not having gone metric yet!

The Mercy convent honey we sampled on cheese and tomato crackers, which worked very well. We were also served honey with clotted cream on the daintiest of scones; the best I have ever tasted, by a long chalk.

Philip, Marie and the Sisters were an absolute joy to work with, coupled with a great sense of humour and real Irish warmth. I can't wait to go back.

July - in mid-summer, when the pollen
is at its best, the honey is more perfumed
and plentiful

CORY'S GRANOLA

I once went fishing in the Tennessee mountains in America with a chef friend of mine, Cory Mattson. We would get up really early and kayak down river with only black coffee and this granola recipe. It has always stood out in my mind as one of the nicest things I have eaten at 4 in the morning; I can still see the river now, covered in early morning mist, great memories. Eaten with yoghurt and milk, it makes a great snack or breakfast, and is very good for you.

Makes: 1.25kg (2¾lb)

250g (9oz) jumbo oats

125g (4½oz) sunflower seeds

125g (4½oz) wheatgerm

200ml (7fl oz) olive oil

200g (7oz) soft light brown sugar

250g (9oz) runny honey

70g (2½oz) each of shelled hazelnuts, pecan nuts, walnuts and flaked almonds

85g (3oz) natural wheat bran

85g (3oz) sultanas

85g (3oz) dried apricots, chopped

85g (3oz) coconut shavings, toasted

100g (3½oz) dried banana chips

1 Preheat the oven to 180°C/350°F/Gas 4. Line two medium baking trays with thick foil.

2 Put the oats, seeds, wheatgerm, olive oil, sugar, honey and nuts into a large mixing bowl and combine well. Spread the mixture thinly over the base of the lined trays. Bake for about 20 minutes, stirring occasionally, until golden brown. Take out of the oven and leave to cool.

3 When cooled, tip into a big bowl and add the rest of the ingredients. Mix well and seal in a container.

FORCED RHUBARB SOUP WITH HONEYCOMB

Rhubarb marries very well with rich savoury foods such as wild and domestic duck, goose, foie gras and even fattier cuts of pork such as belly, collar and my Dad's favourite, pigs' trotters. It's not often you see rhubarb in a soup like this: simple, quick and very pleasing to the eye.

Serves: 4

450g (1lb) forced rhubarb

juice and finely grated zest of 1 unwaxed lime

1 vanilla pod, split

115g (4oz) unrefined golden caster sugar

200ml (7fl oz) dry vermouth

1 honeycomb (jars of honey containing a honeycomb are sold by some supermarkets)

200g (7oz) crème fraîche

1 Roughly chop the rhubarb into chunks, about 3cm (1¼in) is fine.

2 Place the rhubarb, lime zest and juice, vanilla pod and caster sugar into a saucepan. Cook for about 5 minutes with the lid on, so the juices start to run and the rhubarb starts to break down. Add the vermouth, bring to the boil and cook for a further 10 minutes. Liquidize until very smooth, pass through a fine sieve and keep warm.

3 Meanwhile, carefully remove the honeycomb from the jar and cut into small chunks. Add to the crème fraîche and bring together so you can still see the comb in the crème fraîche.

4 To serve, swirl some crème fraîche into the warm soup. If you have a sweet tooth, you may need to add a little more sugar.

SEARED SCALLOPS WITH SPICED GOOSEBERRY KETCHUP

Serves: 4

2 tbsp olive oil

12 large fresh, firm scallops, including roes, shelled and cleaned

sea salt and cracked black pepper

Gooseberry ketchup

450g (1lb) fresh ripe cooking gooseberries

½ tsp hot chilli powder

85g (3oz) caster sugar

20g (¾oz) runny honey

a large pinch of sea salt

125ml (4fl oz) cider wine vinegar

The season for gooseberries is generally mid-June and is a very short one. Apart from in fools and crumbles, you don't often see gooseberries used now, although many years ago the gooseberry was in big demand and several varieties were grown. For this dish I would steer clear of purple, sweet dessert varieties such as Rukola and Whinham's Industry. The balance of the sharp green gooseberries, cider vinegar, honey and chilli is just about right, and works well with sweeter fish, such as scallops or salmon, or with fattier cuts of meat and poultry.

1 Pick over the gooseberries and remove any stalks, then wash well. Place the gooseberries and chilli powder into a stainless-steel pan, add enough water to barely cover the bottom of the pan and cook over a gentle heat until you have a thick stew, about 15 minutes.

2 Liquidize then pass through a fine sieve. Take care not to liquidize for too long or the sauce may turn slightly bitter. Return to the pan and add the sugar, honey, salt and vinegar to the sauce. Bring to the boil and dissolve the sugar then cook down gently until the sauce is thick, similar to double cream. This will take about 20-25 minutes. Use straightaway.

3 Heat a non-stick frying pan, then add the olive oil. Season the scallops well with sea salt and cracked black pepper. Sear on both sides for a couple of minutes. Do not overcook.

4 Serve the scallops with a few sautéed courgette slivers, a couple of tbsp of the gooseberry ketchup and a scattering of chopped chives.

ANIMAL HUSBANDRY
CHEALE'S ABATTOIR

What animals have been reared on, whether they have been raised in a humane or even organic environment, and how long the resulting meat is hung are important questions that we should automatically ask ourselves when we look at meat in our butchers or on the supermarket shelves. Also, I believe we should care greatly about the hastened end of a farm animal's life, which is why I insisted on the inclusion of this page.

I first experienced the great bond a farmer can develop with the animals in his care many years ago when I helped out on a farm over a five-year period. It was only a smallholding, but farmer George King and his son Andrew spent huge amounts of time and effort ensuring their animals were well cared for. This meant more than just providing them with good-quality food; it also meant ensuring that they were clean, happy and warm, especially in the depths of a Kentish coastal winter. Where the idyll ended for the animals, though, used to be at the slaughterhouse. Years ago an abattoir was the stuff of nightmares to me. Although I felt strongly that this section of the book had to be written, I was dreading the trip.

I read some shocking research recently that claimed a fifth of children in Britain don't know where their meat comes from. When surveyed, some even said 'meat is from plastic packets in the supermarket'. To be fair, most people neither know nor want to know what goes on inside the slaughterhouses that provide them with their meat, so I steeled myself to visit the abattoir of the Cheale family and what a pleasant surprise (if that's the right phrase) I had when I got there and was met by Paul Cheale and his son Matthew.

My first impression was that the place was absolutely spotless. Our arrival coincided with that of a large cattle truck. Inside were pigs – lots of them. On closer inspection they seemed very quiet, relaxed and very clean. Paul Cheale explained to me that the trucks were fitted with fans to blow refreshing air over the animals in transit. Once unloaded, the pigs were shepherded into a maze of clean, large holding-pens. When we visited, it was a warm day so all the pigs were being regularly sprayed with cooling water. Some were so relaxed they had even fallen asleep.

From there, the pigs were calmly led into a small pen, where they were stunned with electricity and then dispatched. The killing happens in a way that has probably not changed for thousands of years all over the world. One deft slice to the throat with a sharp knife and the deed is done. I'd venture to guess there's no pain and no awareness from the pig. At no point did the animal looked distressed, unhappy or frightened.

A brisk but thorough process swings into action after that. First, the animals are steamed to soften the bristles before dehairing. The carcasses are singed, brushed, and the innards are removed; then the carcasses are split and the spinal cord extracted. The sides of pork are washed, graded for fat content, weighed and finally hung. Nothing is wasted: heads, lights, ears, tails. To quote the old saying 'everything except the squeak is used'. From start to finish, the process was superbly organized, clean, and, above all, as humane as it could possibly be.

I have to admit, the abattoir is not the sort of place I would want to visit every day, but I'm glad we did. It proves to me, and hopefully you too, that animal welfare, even in a large commercial operation like this, is paramount to its owners. Yes, I will be telling my children about this – I believe I owe it to them.

ADDRESSES

Colin Boswell, The Garlic Farm
Mersley Farm, Newchurch,
Isle of Wight PO36 0NR
Tel: 01983 865378
Fax: 01983 862294
www.thegarlicfarm.co.uk

Brown & Forrest
FREEPOST BS 6843,
Langport, Somerset TA10 0BP
Tel: 01458 250875
Fax: 01458 253475
info@smokedeel.co.uk

Cropwell Bishop Creamery Limited
Cropwell Bishop, Nottinghamshire NG12 3BQ
Tel: +44 (0)115 989 2350
Fax: +44 (0)115 989 9046
www.cropwellbishopstilton.com

Dickinson & Morris
Ye Olde Pork Pie Shoppe,
10 Nottingham Street,
Melton Mowbray,
Leicestershire LE13 1NW
Tel: +44 (0) 1664 482068
Fax: +44 (0) 1664 568052
dickinsonandmorris@porkpie.co.uk

Docwras Rock Shop
13 Regent Road, Great Yarmouth,
Norfolk NR30 2AF
Tel: 01493 844676

F. Duerr & Sons Ltd
Floats Road, Roundthorn Industrial Estate,
Wythenshawe,
Manchester M23 9DR
Tel: 0161 9460535
admin@duerrs.co.uk

Edradour Distillery
Pitlochry, Perthshire PH16 5JP
Tel: (+44) 01796 472 095
Fax: (+44) 01796 472 002
www.edradour.co.uk

Furness Fish & Game Supplies
Moor Lane, Flookburgh, Grange-over-Sands,
Cumbria LA11 7LS
Tel: (+44) 015395 59544
Fax: (+44) 015395 59549
furnessfish@yahoo.com

Peter Gott, Sillfield Farm
Endmoor, Kendal,
Cumbria LA8 0HZ
www.sillfield.co.uk
Tel: 015395 67609

The Grasmere Gingerbread Shop
Church Cottage, Grasmere, Ambleside,
Cumbria LA22 9SW
Tel: +44 (0) 15394 35428
Fax: +44 (0)15394 35155
www.grasmeregingerbread.co.uk

Inverawe Smokehouses
Taynuilt, Argyll PA35 1HU
Tel: 0870 423 0236
Fax: 01866 822274
info@inverawe.co.uk

Mick Jenrick Eels
Shop 18, Stands C1 & C6,
Billingsgate Fish Market,
Isle of Dogs, London E14 5ST
Tel: 020 7987 1118

Philip McCabe
Federation of Irish Beekeepers' Associations
Tel: 00353 (0) 872554854

Marie McGuirk, Home Economist
An Grianán, Termonfechin,
County Louth, Eire
Tel: (0) 41 9822119; (0) 41 9822478

E. Oldroyd & Sons (Lofthouse) Ltd
Hopefield Farm, The Shutts, Leadwell Lane,
Rothwell, Leeds, West Yorkshire LS26 0ST
Tel: 0113 282 2245
www.yorkshirerhubarb.co.uk

A. E. Rodda & Sons
The Creamery, Scorrier, Redruth.
Cornwall TR16 5BU
www.roddas.co.uk

Sarre Mill
Ramsgate Road, Sarre, Near Canterbury,
Kent CT7 0JU
Tel: 01843 847573

Shepherd Neame Brewery
17 Court Street, Faversham,
Kent ME13 7AX
Tel: 01795 542016
www.shepherd-neame.co.uk

R. J. Sheppy & Son
Three Bridges, Bradford on Tone,
Taunton, Somerset TA4 1ER
Tel: 01823 461233
www.sheppycider.com

Trethowan's Dairy Ltd
Gorwydd Farm, Llanddewi Brefi,
Tregaron, Ceredigion SY25 6NY
Office: 01570 493 516
Fax: 01570 493 274
Mobile: 07811 330 140
www.gorwydd.com

The Watercress Company
Waddock Cross, Dorchester,
Dorset DT2 8QY
Tel: 01929 401405
info@thewatercresscompany.com

Wilkin and Sons Ltd
Tiptree, Colchester, Essex CO5 0RF
Tel: 01621 815407
Fax: 01621 814555
www.tiptree.com

INDEX

Entries in **bold** are recipe names.

AUTHOR'S ACKNOWLEDGEMENTS

There are many people to thank. First and foremost, all the producers, growers and beekeepers, without whom I would not have been able to write this book. We turned up at odd times of the year, at odd hours, invariably late, and often after we had cancelled a previous time – so many, many thanks to you all.

Steve Lee, who has done an absolutely stunning job with the photographs. We travelled around the country having great fun, photographing great things and eating them all – wonderful. Not only did I get a great-looking book, I also gained a great friend.

My good friend Simon Whitaker, the director of most of the short films we made with growers and producers for 'This Morning', not only here but all over the world. We met all the people I write about in this book three years ago. Simon is a superb film-maker and author as well, overseeing all my garbled scribbles and placing them in some sort of order.

Julia Alger, my long-serving home economist. A great job again; here's to the next one.

Bea Harling, Nestlé developer. A fab job, you're one of the best around.

Becca Spry, for believing in the original idea and never hassling me. Miranda Harvey for the great design and understanding exactly what I wanted. Susan Fleming, the best in the business.

John Rush, friend, and my agent Luigi Bonomi, the best around, for getting me in front of the right people at the right time.

Too many friends to thank for tasting, tasting and tasting again: Karen, Anthony, Dan, Becca, Carol, Charlotte, Tim, Sue... For giving me great inspiration, Paul Vidic, chef and friend of 27 years, Andy Knight, my chef when we opened the brasserie (but who still can't cook bass), Steve Poole, a pretty fine cook (claims he taught me all I know).

Peter Gott, for teaching me the secrets of bacon curing and drinking too much Guinness, and Christine for putting us up and cooking great food.

Finally, to my wife Fern, thank you for everything.

PHOTOGRAPHER'S ACKNOWLEDGEMENTS

Phil and I travelled the length and breadth of the country to produce this book, shooting thousands of images throughout the seasons. We worked hard, yet had tremendous fun. Thanks for the friendship, Phil.

I met so many wonderful people that made this journey so special. You know who you are – thank you.

To my three sons Douglas, Sonny and Charlie who put up with me being away from home so much, and to Jan. You are the best mother to them.

Tony – thanks mate – for looking after the Studio in my absence.

Miranda – you have done a magnificent job with your design.

I would like to dedicate this book to my father, John Lee, who in his heyday was one of London's finest food photographers. Thanks, Dad, you taught me so much.